Spiritual Interviews
with the
Guardian Spirits of

BIDEN
and
TRUMP

RYUHO OKAWA

HS PRESS

Copyright © 2020 by Ryuho Okawa
English translation © Happy Science 2020
Original title: *Beidaitoryosen Biden Koho to
Trump Koho no Shugorei Interview*
HS Press is an imprint of IRH Press Co., Ltd.
Tokyo
ISBN 13: 978-1-943869-92-3
ISBN 10: 1-943869-92-8
Cover Image: EPA=JIJI
Zack Stock Photo/shutterstock.com
Jaws_73/shutterstock.com

*No statements made by the guardian spirits of Mr. Joseph Biden and
Mr. Donald Trump in this book reflect statements actually made by themselves.*

*The opinions of the spirits in this book do not necessarily reflect
those of Happy Science Group.
For the mechanism behind spiritual messages, see the end section.*

Contents

Preface 11

PROLOGUE

Spiritually Interviewing the Guardian Spirits of Biden and Trump regarding the Upcoming Presidential Election

It's time to touch on the presidential election 14

Military operations and other classified information must
remain top secret 15

First, a spiritual interview with the guardian spirit of
Biden 17

CHAPTER ONE

Spiritual Interview with the Guardian Spirit of Joe Biden

1 Finding Out How Biden Thinks

Summoning the guardian spirit of Biden, the former vice president under Obama 24

Biden's guardian spirit on alert as he is summoned for the first time 25

Waiting for Trump to make a big mistake 29

"I am decent as a human being" 32

Asking about illegal immigrants and racism 36

The topic of Chinese affairs during his vice presidency is "inconvenient for me" 40

2 Biden's Pro-Chinese Philosophy Might Mean He Acknowledges Hegemonism

"The Spratly Islands problem is not an issue" 45

Way of negotiation may change regarding the Hong Kong problem 46

He has no intention of going to war with 1.4 billion people in order to save 7 million 49

It's delusional for China to aim to take Hawaii 52

He thinks in terms of "balance of interests," not "human rights" and "freedom" 53

He sees the Senkaku Islands dispute as a food and energy problem 57

"Hong Kong is small. In order to support the U.S. economy, we cannot lose a market of 1.4 billion people" 59

Biden lacks a sense of urgency believing that "There's no way China will ever catch up with the U.S." 62

Just like former President Obama, he is considering pacifism with the goal of a nuclear-free world 65

3 How Does He See the Country of Japan?

"I don't mind if there's a war between the U.S. and China, but I want to limit the battlefield to at furthest Japan" 67

His awareness of the science and technology competition with China 69

China is expanding its military for defensive purpose 71

President Trump is now trying to crush China's ambition of becoming no. 1 in the world in 2040 73

He leaks his true feelings about Japan, Taiwan, and Hong Kong 75

Asking about Biden's health problems 78

4 Discovering the True Nature of Biden's Soul

His previous life was as a sheriff in the old west, and two-lives ago was as a slave trader 82

In a past life, he was a Jesuit missionary preaching in China 85

Who guides Biden's guardian spirit? 90

He protests the nickname "Sleepy Joe" 94

5 **Asking His Views on the Novel Coronavirus That Originated in China**

He wants to hold President Trump more responsible for
the coronavirus problem than China 96

He intends to withdraw the nuclear weapons on U.S.
military bases in Asia to Guam and Hawaii 100

CHAPTER TWO

Spiritual Interview with the Guardian Spirit of Donald Trump

1 **President Trump's Chances of Being Reelected**

Interview with Biden's guardian spirit should just be an appendix 106

The media attacks President Trump because he's powerful 108

Trumponomics and *Trump-Keizai-Kakumei* can save Japan 110

Biden will lose because his economic policy is bad 112

2 **The Course for Containing Dictatorial China**

Hong Kong's chief executive may not live to see the New Year 114

"I can use a fleet of five nations, but Biden can't use the British army" 115

What it means to normalize diplomatic relations between Israel and the UAE 117

"I want to turn Iran into a democracy and stabilize the Middle East" 119

On President Trump's North Korea diplomacy 120

China wants to strike down the American economy 121

We'll keep Japan and Taiwan's damages to a minimum 124

"I will be reelected and bring about Xi Jinping's downfall within two years" 127

The basic strategy: cause an internal conflict among the
central powers and divide their opinions 129

We cannot fight China unless Trump is reelected as
"wartime president" 130

3 **Prospects for the Presidential Election and China's
Democratization**

"If it looks like Biden will win, God will use His lightning
of rage" 134

We've already simulated the Taiwan crisis 138

China's military training in the South China Sea is a
diversion 140

"There is no way China can attack Japan's U.S. military
bases first" 141

Japan's ultimate weapon against the CCP 144

China's post-Xi democratization 145

Stay still before you attack 146

Mail-in ballots could lead to a rigged election 148

China's real vital point that Biden cannot resolve 150

4 **Expectations for Happy Science**

Systems that uphold freedom, democracy, and faith should
be kept mainstream in the world 153

Pro-Chinese politicians in Japan and their corruption
scandals 156

Trump overcame obstacles with his never-give-up spirit and
positive thinking 158

"Master Ryuho Okawa and I are fellow heroes, we think
alike" 161

The connection between God Shiva and President Trump 162

"Write 'God chose Mr. Trump as the president of the U.S.' on the wraparound band" 164

Trump's G.S. believes he is God's right hand or left hand 167

What a Japanese leader must be able to say 168

5　**The Words of God: "The Current Chinese Regime Will Fall"** 172

Afterword 175

About the Author 177

What is El Cantare? 178

What is a Spiritual Message? 180

About Happy Science 184

About Happy Science Movies 188

Contact Information 190

About Happiness Realization Party 192

About IRH Press 193

Books by Ryuho Okawa 194

In this book, there are a total of four interviewers from Happy Science, symbolized as A, B, C, and D, in the order that they first appear.

Preface

The U.S. presidential election is coming up, and it's a head-to-head race between Mr. Biden, the Democrat, and Mr. Trump, the Republican.

Biden of the U.S. Democratic Party is avoiding making public appearances and waiting for Trump to make a slip of the tongue. This seems to be his strategy.

To begin with, it was anticipated that Trump would win a landslide victory if it weren't for the major disaster brought upon by the coronavirus.

But the U.S. has become the worst affected country in the world, with nearly six million infected and well over 100,000 dead. And now, their mass media predict that the Democrat, Biden, has the advantage.

Biden served as vice president of the Obama administration, during which China overtook Japan in GDP, and that has led to an increased risk of a hegemonic war between the U.S. and China. In this book, we closed in on the true thoughts of both candidates to get a forecast of the U.S. presidential election, in the form of a spiritual interview with their guardian spirits. We hope you will read and see their differences.

Ryuho Okawa
Master & CEO of Happy Science Group
August 19, 2020

PROLOGUE

Spiritually Interviewing the Guardian Spirits of Biden and Trump regarding the Upcoming Presidential Election

*Originally recorded in Japanese on August 17, 2020,
in the Special Lecture Hall of Happy Science in Japan,
and later translated into English.*

It's time to touch on the presidential election

RYUHO OKAWA

Good morning.

I believe it is about time to touch on the U.S. presidential election. It is a showdown between the Democratic candidate Biden and the Republican candidate Trump.

Mr. Trump's guardian spirit has given us spiritual messages several times and Mr. Trump himself has voiced various opinions, so I think that many people understand his position. However, I think that the people including the Japanese feel less informed about Mr. Biden.

This should, in fact, be done in English, but I considered the fact that detailed points and subtle nuances may not be conveyed well, so I decided to do this in Japanese.

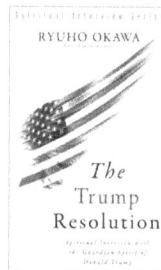

The Trump Secret (New York: IRH Press, 2017), *The Trump Resolution* (Tokyo: HS Press, 2018)

Also, looking at the recent distribution of my *Kuro-Obi Eigo* (lit. "Black Belt in English") series, I can determine that there are not even 2,000 Japanese members who would understand English at this level, and since that would be a waste, I would like to do this in a simultaneous interpretation form in Japanese.

If there are words or phrases that cannot be translated into Japanese, there is a possibility that some English will be used, but I think I can interpret most of them. I did an experiment with Mr. Trump the other day and there were no issues.

I have never spoken to Mr. Biden's guardian spirit, so I am not sure how it will be, but since Mr. Biden's English is not that easy to understand either, I would like to do my best to do this in Japanese.

Military operations and other classified information must remain top secret

RYUHO OKAWA

In the U.S., it is about time they begin to criticize each other back and forth, so neither of their guardian spirits wants to reveal all of the cards they have in their hand. It is now mid-August and there may be cards they would want to hold until around October, so they may not want to talk about those and end up expressing things vaguely.

Also, this may be mainly from Mr. Trump's side, but if he is thinking of some kind of military operation, that would be top secret. Even if I do this spiritual interview in Japan, it is highly possible that the information would be sent to countries of concern in about a day. If it is in English, it could be the same day and even if it is in Japanese, if there is someone that understands Japanese, it can be conveyed.

If we do this in English, Mr. Trump would say things too straightforwardly and it is highly possible that the conclusion would be revealed. So, I think it might be safe to filter his opinions by simultaneously interpreting to Japanese and make sure that things he shouldn't be saying will not be revealed.

It is possible that the questioner Mr. A may ask persistently, so Mr. Trump may be prompted to answer if asked. However, in the case of a military operation, the U.S. would most likely not inform even Japan, which is an ally, until about an hour before the action. So, even if he answers, if I feel some of them shouldn't be open to the public, I may use a vague expression in Japanese.

Mr. Trump's guardian spirit has been extremely careful from around this March to August and has not come to me. There are other spirits who have mentioned that he thinks he will be forced to talk if he comes, so I think that is the case. Therefore, you can ask, but it is highly possible that the answer may not be accurate.

Aide to Master & CEO told me three times this morning, "A secret is a secret, so please don't reveal it." I have a habit of talking straightforwardly too, so I would like to be careful as well. Still, I would like you to ask what the general public wishes to hear.

First, a spiritual interview with the guardian spirit of Biden

RYUHO OKAWA

Now, if I do Mr. Trump first and then Mr. Biden, it may be unfavorable for Mr. Trump, so I believe we should do Mr. Biden first, then have Mr. Trump speak if he has any rebuttal. This will be slightly favorable to him. So, I wish to start with Mr. Biden, who we have not had a session with yet.

I am not sure if I can interpret it into Japanese, but I think it will work. You can ask things if it is in Japanese, right?

A
Yes.

RYUHO OKAWA
If you ask in English, you may find it hard to ask questions to Mr. Biden's guardian spirit, right?

A
Yes.

RYUHO OKAWA
Yes, that's one reason.

A
Mr. Biden seems to speak nonsense in his interviews, too.

RYUHO OKAWA
It might be so. It would not be good if he embarrasses himself and is suspected of dementia. If he does, please take it as bad translation.

Well, then I would like to interview the guardian spirits of the candidates, Mr. Biden and Mr. Trump, in connection with the presidential election.

CHAPTER ONE

Spiritual Interview with the Guardian Spirit of Joe Biden

*Originally recorded in Japanese on August 17, 2020,
in the Special Lecture Hall of Happy Science in Japan,
and later translated into English.*

Joseph Robinette Biden, Jr. (1942 - Present)

An American politician. Democrat. Born in Pennsylvania. He graduated from the University of Delaware and Syracuse University College of Law. Biden was first elected to the Senate in 1972, at the age of 29, and served a total of six terms. He dropped out of the presidential primaries in 1988 after being accused of plagiarizing a British politician's speech. In 2008, he ran again for the presidential election and was defeated. Obama nominated Biden as his running mate, eventually making Biden the vice president for two terms until January 2017. Commonly known as Joe Biden.

1

Finding Out How Biden Thinks

Summoning the guardian spirit of Biden, the former vice president under Obama

RYUHO OKAWA

First is Mr. Joseph Biden, who was the vice president under President Obama's administration for eight years. Having served in the previous administration, he of course has opposing thoughts to Mr. Trump and knows all about the Obama administration. The reason why he remained a candidate is that he can be immediately effective as he was recently the vice president, and hence he would be able to start his administration fairly quickly.

Well then, I will call him.

[*Claps once.*] Mr. Joseph Biden, the guardian spirit of Mr. Joe Biden.

[*While clapping slowly and softly.*] Please come to Happy Science in Japan. Please allow me to deliver your spiritual message in Japanese through my simultaneous interpretation.

Mr. Joe Biden, Mr. Joe Biden. Presidential candidate, Mr. Joe Biden of the Democratic Party. Please answer us.

[*About 10 seconds of silence.*]

Biden's guardian spirit on alert as he is summoned for the first time

JOE BIDEN'S GUARDIAN SPIRIT
Hmm.

A
Good morning.

BIDEN'S G.S.
Ah. Morning!

A
Good morning. Is this Mr. Joe Biden's guardian spirit?

BIDEN'S G.S.
Yes.

A

Thank you very much for coming today, despite your busy schedule for the presidential election.

BIDEN'S G.S.

Wha... What is this?

A

This is a Japanese religious organization, Happy Science, which is also in the U.S. and around the world. As a religion, we are now calling on Mr. Joe Biden's guardian spirit.

BIDEN'S G.S.

Uh-huh. Oh, I see. Hmm, OK.

A

We would like you to talk freely about various comments against Trump or global issues as you approach the presidential election.

BIDEN'S G.S.

Uh-huh. Oh, I have the impression that you guys have a strong pro-Trump sentiment.

A

We would like to ask you from a neutral position today.

BIDEN'S G.S.

Really? I hope so. If you are trying to prove I am incompetent and show that to the Japanese people...

B

No, rather...

BIDEN'S G.S.

Huh?

B

...it is an opportunity to promote to Japan and the world how wonderful Mr. Biden is, so please...

BIDEN'S G.S.

Is that so? You are a good man.

B

Thank you [*laughs*].

BIDEN'S G.S.

Good, good. You are a good guy.

B

We...

BIDEN'S G.S.

[*To A.*] You are scary. A little.

B

[*Laughs.*] We would appreciate it if you could tell us your true thoughts.

A

And today, we have remotely connected Mr. C.

BIDEN'S G.S.

The guy that translated a terrible book* about Mr. Trump.

A

Terrible book?

---

* Here, the guardian spirit of Biden is referring to: Stephen Moore, and Arthur B Laffer, *Trumponomics*, trans. Motohisa Fujii (Tokyo: IRH Press, 2019).

BIDEN'S G.S.

Yes.

C

Hello. I would like to hear your honest thoughts.

BIDEN'S G.S.

No, I will never support you. That's not going to happen. I am against you.

Waiting for Trump to make a big mistake

A

Well then, we will go into details.

Initially, before the coronavirus issue, it was said that Mr. Trump will have an overwhelming victory.

BIDEN'S G.S.

Yes, OK. Maybe? OK. Yes.

A

But now, the situation has been reversed and you are considered to have a definite win.

BIDEN'S G.S.

Hahaha. Oh, you, you, you.

A

[*Laughs.*]

BIDEN'S G.S.

You, you, you must be a very tricky person [*laughs*].

A

No [*laughs*]. Why do you think so?

BIDEN'S G.S.

You know [*laughs*], there are many people like you among news anchors at TV stations. They lift you up and smash you to the ground. I know that tactic, I know. Don't try it on me.

A

No, no, this is not my subjective opinion. The American media is saying so.

BIDEN'S G.S.

Oh, is that so? I see.

A

Your approval ratings are more than 10 points higher.

BIDEN'S G.S.

You cannot tell yet. Not yet. No. If I declared victory now, I would be destroyed.

A

Then, who do you think will be the president at this point?

BIDEN'S G.S.

Oh [*laughs*], that is very tough to answer. Very difficult. How should I answer? Hmm.

The reason why my approval ratings are high is that they include the criticism against Trump and his administration now. So, if Mr. Trump changes his policy in response to the criticisms, that part of the votes will shift to him. That is why it is not certain that I will win. Mr. Trump has things he can still do as president but has not accomplished. If he takes those actions, the votes will shift to him, so there is still a possibility that he will win. I am doing my best to advocate what Mr. Trump has not done. If he takes action, the votes will shift, so there is nothing definite yet.

We are working as we go and things change according to the opponent. So, honestly, there will be less damage for me if I say that I'm not sure who will win.

A

I see. I understand. In short, you are getting points now because of Trump's failure.

BIDEN'S G.S.

Of course, I'm waiting for him to make a big mistake.

A

So, objectively, that's how you are thinking.

BIDEN'S G.S.

Yes, yes.

"I am decent as a human being"

A

Then, what is the greatest strength you can appeal to the American people?

BIDEN'S G.S.

I am decent as a human being.

A

Decent as a human being?

BIDEN'S G.S.

This is my greatest strength.

A

I see.

BIDEN'S G.S.

Mr. Trump is like Joker from the Batman series serving as the president. Everyone thinks so. It is so obvious. I'm decent.

A

Decent.

BIDEN'S G.S.

He is the Joker.

A

By decent, do you mean your character?

BIDEN'S G.S.

As a human being, everyone from God to animals sees me as decent.

A

But a president must produce results or accomplish something.

BIDEN'S G.S.

Well, this is difficult. Even in the Batman series, some of their box office revenues total about $1 billion without Joker and also when Joker is the leading role. The box office of the series does well regardless of good or evil.

In terms of votes, it is possible that you can get votes if people are interested in you, regardless of good or bad.

A

I guess so.

BIDEN'S G.S.

I am not sure what kind of strange things he will do to attack me, but the more crazy it looks, the more amused people will be and the more people will vote for him.

A

Sure. That's in the world of entertainment, but in the world of politics, whether you will make the right decision is the big factor.

BIDEN'S G.S.

You cannot tell whether you are right or not. The result of the election is everything.

A

No, no, no. What kind of decisions will you make when you become president?

BIDEN'S G.S.

The last time, Hillary was defeated. It was unexpected.

What Trump said was to create a wall on the border of Mexico, which just sounds crazy based on common sense. He is a crazy president. The words of a crazy president are too easy to understand. Build a fence on the border of Mexico at their cost? That's just cartoonish. It's absurd. Unfair. Usually...

A

But he really built it.

BIDEN'S G.S.

It's absurd, but it is easy to understand. Very easy to understand. Especially for people who are suffering from the spread of drug crimes near the Mexican border, this seemingly crazy act begins to look like reality because it's visible.

Asking about illegal immigrants and racism

A

OK, shall we go there? Do you think illegal immigrants should be allowed in the U.S. or not?

BIDEN'S G.S.

Mr. Trump is basically a racist, so I think he thinks everyone is an illegal immigrant, except for white Americans. He probably thinks they are illegal immigrants but are allowed to enter under certain conditions. His racist views are very deep-rooted.

A

Then, you think there is nothing wrong with illegal immigrants.

BIDEN'S G.S.

Those who are newly educated in the U.S. and making an effort to be an American citizen have the possibility to be a U.S. citizen.

A

But illegal immigration is also a hotbed of crime, isn't it?

BIDEN'S G.S.

That's because the police are lazy.

A

The police are lazy?

BIDEN'S G.S.

Yes. The police are slacking off.

A

But the states where the governors are democrats are preventing the police from doing their work.

BIDEN'S G.S.

That's not true. In that case, Schwarzenegger will go and fight on his own. It's OK.

A

What do you think should be done about the issue with African Americans now? I mean, the ongoing riots.

[*Something makes a noise in the ceiling.*]

BIDEN'S G.S.

Does this place have poltergeists?

A

[*Laughs.*]

BIDEN'S G.S.

I just heard the sound of a poltergeist opposing me from the ceiling.

A

So, are you for or against Black Lives Matter?

BIDEN'S G.S.

Well, that was something convenient that happened at a convenient time... or inconvenient? That was something inconvenient for him. Information disclosure has become so advanced in the U.S. I feel sorry for Mr. Trump.

An African American was held down on his neck by the knee of a police officer until he died from suffocation. That was caught live on video and broadcasted. That was a rare incident where the police were at fault. If such a thing is released and people watch it on the news over and over again, it becomes clear how things are unfavorable for African Americans.

So, I do feel sorry for Mr. Trump. Poor thing. I think he was abandoned by the heavens.

A

You are also famous for giving racist remarks from time to time.

BIDEN'S G.S.

No, it says I am well-versed in international affairs... According to the information you have, it says here that I am known as the greatest internationalist in U.S. politics, so that's not the case.

The topic of Chinese affairs during his vice presidency is "inconvenient for me"

A

Then, may I talk about international issues and foreign affairs?

You served as the chairman of the Senate's Foreign Affairs Committee, and your strongest point is said to be in diplomacy. However, just before the presidential primaries, it was said that Mr. Biden would be unable to be president and that if he were to be the candidate, Mr. Trump would definitely win. This was because, in fact, the Bidens had a worse corruption structure than the Clintons in Ukraine and China.

BIDEN'S G.S.

[*Clears throat.*] You, your words sting.

A

Oh, but this is not my idea, either. It's information that the general mass media has.

BIDEN'S G.S.

You just spoke of the Clintons like you speak of Dracula and his family.

A

Your son's company has been gaining enormous wealth.

BIDEN'S G.S.

You won't be able to run for president in the U.S. without money.

A

First, I'll talk about China. In China, your son and a subsidiary company of the Bank of China created an investment company as a joint venture. Then, after you visited China, a huge sum of money was transferred to that investment company.

BIDEN'S G.S.

Wouldn't it have been better to do this in English after all? You're saying all you want in Japanese.

It's not good.

A

A huge amount of money was transferred two weeks after your visit.

BIDEN'S G.S.

Well, there must be some appreciation.

A

What kind of...

BIDEN'S G.S.

That is the natural thing as a human being, isn't it?

A

You met Mr. Xi Jinping, didn't you?

BIDEN'S G.S.

That is, you know... If he can see me, any amount, he can...

A

Why did that happen?

BIDEN'S G.S.

Why... [*Laughs.*] Speak in English.

A

[*Laughs.*]

BIDEN'S G.S.

This is inconvenient for me. I hope you will be asking Trump similar questions. You know? There are allegations against him of fraudulent admission, so do it.

A

Then, Mr. C will...

BIDEN'S G.S.

I mean, never mind. It's OK.

A

Mr. C wants to speak to you.

BIDEN'S G.S.

Never mind. Well, it's natural for politicians to receive what they are given. I directly...

If I were part of the administration and could manipulate things to benefit China, then it can be criticized as bribery, but this is something that happened when we were not in such a relationship. It's just a favor. A favor.

2

Biden's Pro-Chinese Philosophy Might Mean He Acknowledges Hegemonism

"The Spratly Islands problem is not an issue"

A

When you were in charge of foreign affairs under the Obama administration, you and Obama kept silent about China intensifying its territorial activities on the Spratly Islands in the South China Sea.

BIDEN'S G.S.

Hmm. Those were times when the military costs were too high and we had to cut down the budget. We couldn't immediately start a war for something so small.

A

Something so small? Right now, Secretary of State Pompeo is saying that this was a clear violation of international law...

BIDEN'S G.S.

Pompeo wants to waste taxes.

A

Then, how will you handle today's China?

BIDEN'S G.S.

The issue of the Spratly Islands is only that Taiwan, the Philippines, and Vietnam are feeling scared about it.

A

No big deal?

BIDEN'S G.S.

Right, it's not an issue.

Way of negotiation may change regarding the Hong Kong problem

C

I think that the world is paying attention to the situation in Hong Kong.

BIDEN'S G.S.

Ah, uh-huh. Yes, yes.

C

Do you have any idea how you will deal with this?

BIDEN'S G.S.

Ah, ah.

C

Hong Kong's citizens already held demonstrations of one million and two million people last year, and the Communist Party of China is showing their oppression. If you were the American president, how would you respond?

BIDEN'S G.S.

Officially, both Republicans and Democrats have agreed, as a country, to protect Hong Kong's freedom and democracy, so basically, I would say to the public, the same thing as what Mr. Trump... no, Mr. Obama would say if he gave a speech.

However, how much we would actually be involved, or whether we would do things in a violent and fighting manner like Mr. Trump, throwing down harsh tariffs, may differ. The methods and ways of negotiation may change, but the official idea, I think, would be the same, as we are American.

A

The official idea?

BIDEN'S G.S.

Yes.

C

Do you mean your real thoughts are different?

BIDEN'S G.S.

In fact, it is hard to say whether what Mr. Trump is doing with sanctions and various methods will really end as just an economic matter or if he is provoking China.

B

So, under the Biden administration, do you plan to stop the current U.S.-China war on trade, tariffs, and intellectual property?

BIDEN'S G.S.

Well, I wouldn't say that, but as much as possible, I do want to choose to take a stance so that the U.S. contributes to world peace. So, I am not going to focus only on American interests and proclaim "America First" like Trump. Instead, I want to start negotiating in a way that enables us to maintain world peace.

He has no intention of going to war with 1.4 billion people in order to save 7 million

B

This Hong Kong issue is not a problem that concerns Hong Kong alone. Neither is it a domestic issue as asserted by China. Rather, it's a global issue about freedom, which is also one of the founding philosophies of the U.S.

A military option is another card in President Trump's hand that he could play, while China is trying to forcibly stamp out the freedoms held by Hong Kong citizens by use of military force.

BIDEN'S G.S.

Sure. I guess so. That's why this election is so important. The choice between Trump and Biden will determine whether or not the Chinese will face numerous casualties.

I think that it is important to protect the 7 million people (in Hong Kong) and that protecting the rights of minorities is a form of democracy. But I do not think it would be a good idea to start a world war against a country with 1.4 billion people.

B

What you're trying to say is if you become president, in regard to the Hong Kong issue, military action will...

BIDEN'S G.S.

No, quite the opposite. I would probably urge China—Beijing government—to take a softer stance toward Hong Kong by enticing them with some sort of benefit.

A

What do you mean by enticing them with some sort of benefit?

BIDEN'S G.S.

For example, Trump has imposed harsh economic sanctions, and has done other things that affect some Chinese officials' honor, such as freezing the assets of the people allegedly involved in various acts of oppression, right? In other words, he is treating China in the same way that Iraq was treated before and in the same way that Iran is being treated right now. And North Korea as well. Trump is treating China in the same way as North Korea, Iran, and Iraq. I am sure that wounds their pride.

A

You mean that you will lift economic sanctions, right?

BIDEN'S G.S.

No, I'm not saying that. Well, whether I lift them or not would be determined through negotiations with China. I might try to negotiate a bit more like, "If you cease military actions and stop so severely disadvantaging or oppressing the people of Hong Kong, giving them no choice but to flee, then I might review the sanctions somewhat." That would be a way of stopping the oppression through economic pressure. If I were to take a hardline approach like Trump, there's no telling how far-reaching the effects would be.

It's delusional for China to aim to take Hawaii

A

A moment ago, you mentioned that you don't think the South China Sea is much of a problem. Does that mean we should now consider it to be China's belonging?

BIDEN'S G.S.

Well, you might consider it a loss, but China wants to build bases there and fish there, right?

A

Are you saying that China is expanding into the region in order to catch fish?

BIDEN'S G.S.

It's mostly about fishing rights, isn't it? Their 1.4 billion people have to eat. So, it makes sense that they have to expand their territorial waters in order to catch enough fish.

A

But their long-term maritime strategy includes breaking through the first island chain and the second island chain, and ultimately, they even have their eyes on Hawaii...

BIDEN'S G.S.

Oh, I've heard about that, but I don't believe it.

A

You don't believe it?

BIDEN'S G.S.

The idea of them "coming to take Hawaii" is [*laughs*]. America won't just sit by and let that happen. That's delusional. Delusional. It's just a fantasy.

He thinks in terms of "balance of interests," not "human rights" and "freedom"

B

So, are you saying that you do not believe that China will ever actually occupy the territories of other countries through military expansion?

BIDEN'S G.S.

No, I'm not saying that it will never happen. Since I'm also a lawyer, I look at things in terms of what you could call "balance of interests." You have to balance what you stand to lose and what you stand to gain. Take the Senkaku Islands in Japan as an example. Let's assume that the Senkaku Islands are taken by China. In response, as Japan's allied force, the U.S. has to mobilize in order to defend Japan, but if doing so would result in China launching a nuclear missile into Tokyo, then regaining the Senkaku Islands would not be worth it...

This issue is about fishing rights, and also about the possibility of subterranean oil fields in the area, but it would take a long time to succeed at extracting it. That's still 10 to 20 years away.

C
This seems...

BIDEN'S G.S.
Huh?

C
Never mind. Sorry.

BIDEN'S G.S.
Go ahead.

C

This seems more like an issue of values rather than an issue of balance of interests.

BIDEN'S G.S.

Oh, really? Hmm...

C

What I mean is, the Beijing government is a totalitarian state ruled under a one-party dictatorship of the communist party. Inside China, human rights are suppressed, and there is no freedom of speech. How do you feel about that situation? Do you approve of it, object to it, or do you feel that it can be tolerated?

BIDEN'S G.S.

Well, I know how you feel, but right now, China introduced a market economy that contains elements of the socialist planned economy, and the country has undoubtedly become wealthier than it used to be. Although I understand that about half of the population of the country still lives in poverty. When China cracks down on or arrests specific activists, people might call it out as suppressing human rights, but there are still at least 600 million people in China who live in poverty. If their standard of living rises, it will in turn alleviate the misery experienced by Chinese people.

In that sense, I think it is better for China to maintain friendly relations or trade relations with the rest of the world in order to improve its economy further. I mean, if we approach them like they are an enemy that we want to fight... well, Trump's strategy is to isolate China, but while some people in China may be wealthy and elite, his strategy will make it all the more difficult for others who are living in poverty to eat.

Those fish from the South China Sea too. They are not just for the elite in Beijing, but for other people to eat too. They need to have enough money to be able to buy fish. Although they may not be eating the kinds of luxury fish that Japanese people eat.

[*An electrical noise can be heard.*]

There seem to be a lot of poltergeists getting in the way today.

He sees the Senkaku Islands dispute as a food and energy problem

A

Back on the topic of the Senkaku Islands, this is one of the reasons why Japan is in a conflict with China. What would you do if China were to occupy them?

BIDEN'S G.S.

Well, if Japan thinks that its sovereignty extends to the islands, then at the very least, the Japan Self-Defense Forces should engage in defensive activities to drive the occupiers out. If the Self-Defense Forces won't mobilize, then there is no reason why the U.S. military should go there and start a war.

A

You're right.

BIDEN'S G.S.

Yeah. If Japan has sovereignty, then the Self-Defense Forces should be the ones to get rid of the intruders. It's a type of police action, and I'm sure that Japan has that level of capability to do it. If Japan decides not to fight for the Senkaku Islands out of fear of possible friction with China, then there is no reason that the U.S. military would have to go so far as to threaten Beijing and demand that they give it back.

A

So, you basically think that it's probably just about fishing rights?

BIDEN'S G.S.

It's either fishing rights, or there is the possibility of a few submarine oil fields. But people would have to drill to know for sure.

A

And are you saying that, if that's all it's about, then we should let them have it?

BIDEN'S G.S.

Well, right now, China is greedy for food and energy. But that's understandable. I'm sure they need them. It's impossible to conduct industrial activities without energy.

"Hong Kong is small. In order to support the U.S. economy, we cannot lose a market of 1.4 billion people"

A

On the topic of whether or not the U.S. itself will suffer any damage, it has been nearly confirmed that China is funding Black Lives Matter behind the scenes.

BIDEN'S G.S.

Hmm... That's...

A

I am sure that the Democratic Party is involved in it too.

BIDEN'S G.S.

It's easy for people to say things like that. It's easy to spread those kinds of rumors.

A

There is also the TikTok issue. Demonstrators already know the names, family structures, and everything else about the federal officials in charge of public order and security, and they are threatening and attacking them. They know quite a bit about America's personnel allocation. China is maneuvering behind the scenes. Much information is stolen and if nothing is done about it, there is even the possibility that the U.S. will be overthrown.

BIDEN'S G.S.
Oh, what's more likely is...

A
The question is if it gets to that point, will you still support China?

BIDEN'S G.S.
Well, ever since Clinton... I mean, not Hillary Clinton but President Clinton was in office, their international students working at companies and research institutions in the U.S. have been stealing information, and we have known about it since then.

A
So, you knew about it.

BIDEN'S G.S.

It's because we are a big country and an advanced nation. China is less-developed, so they have no choice but to steal information. But even Japan stole lots of information from the U.S.—through students sent to study in the U.S. after WWII.

I used to think that it cannot be helped, but now that China has started to close in on and catch up with us, it has become a problem. Also, America's growth rate has dropped, so...

A

In other words, is your basic idea that, if you take a conciliatory attitude to China and establish a relationship with it, then you will be able to get along well with China?

BIDEN'S G.S.

Yeah. It would be wasteful otherwise. They are a huge market, and in order to support the U.S. economy, we must not lose a market of 1.4 billion people. Hong Kong is small, so by negotiating a way to manage things that is more profitable overall, I think we can negotiate a way for them to live a little more peacefully.

Biden lacks a sense of urgency believing that "There's no way China will ever catch up with the U.S."

A

Although you might call it peaceful, they are stealing technologies from U.S. companies and commercializing them. What do you think is Mr. Xi Jinping's hidden intentions? In your understanding, what does Mr. Xi Jinping want to do?

BIDEN'S G.S.

Well, to him, I am sure that the U.S. has become the target that he wants to catch up with and surpass.

A

So, you think that Mr. Xi Jinping just wants to catch up with and surpass the U.S.?

BIDEN'S G.S.

But there is no way that they will ever catch up.

A

They will never?

BIDEN'S G.S.

I don't think they will ever catch up.

A

They won't?

BIDEN'S G.S.

No. I don't think they will ever catch up with us scientifically or technologically. I'm not worried about that at all. There is ultimately no way that they will ever catch up.

A

However, the key military technologies in the future will be AI and semiconductors. And when it comes to semiconductors, China has already nearly caught up with the U.S. in military technology applications. In the future, in terms of U.S. military power, if you don't have better semiconductors and these other technologies, China will surpass you at some point. You will be left completely powerless.

BIDEN'S G.S.

No, you say that, but it is completely unimaginable that the Chinese military will ever actually be able to come and attack mainland America.

A

No, you won't even be able to intercept their missiles, and in terms of cyber-warfare...

B

There is a war going on already. It's just taking place in unconventional forms, including cyber-warfare, space warfare, economic warfare, and financial warfare. America's wealth is actually being stolen by China.

BIDEN'S G.S.

Yeah, yeah, yeah.

A

China is already stealing technologies and intellectual properties from the U.S. And President Trump is trying to stop them.

BIDEN'S G.S.

But China possesses a large quantity of U.S. government bonds. They constitute a part of their savings. If we should enter into a state of war like that, all of those bonds would definitely be frozen.

Just like former President Obama, he is considering pacifism with the goal of a nuclear-free world

B

You mentioned a moment ago that it will be possible to somehow deal with China through negotiations and that it is a matter of balance of interests, but where is your "red line," the line that you feel should never be crossed?

BIDEN'S G.S.

Well, I was the vice-president in the former Obama administration, so I inherited some of his ideas, and right now at least, I want to consider pacifism with the goal of a nuclear-free world. If we don't aim for that, then we will just keep escalating militarily in the opposite direction. That's why I want to achieve that to the best I can.

There are many Chinese people living in the U.S. too. The U.S. is the sort of nation where people from all sorts of countries can enjoy prosperity. So, if the deep-rooted feelings of racism inside Trump are causing the war, then it is probably God's will that we cut those feelings out from the roots.

A

However, you were also accused of racism by Senator Kamala Harris, your vice-presidential running mate.

BIDEN'S G.S.

I'm sure she wouldn't claim that now.

A

Well, of course, she won't now, but in her heart, she thinks that you are a racist, doesn't she?

BIDEN'S G.S.

Hmm, that was… Hmm… Both Trump and his wife are immigrants, or the descendants of immigrants, whereas I am actually among the U.S. elite. I am genuinely elite. So, there may be people who claim that I am discriminating upon seeing that.

3

How Does He See the Country of Japan?

"I don't mind if there's a war between the U.S. and China, but I want to limit the battlefield to at furthest Japan"

C

I would like to ask a question as a Japanese person. From listening to you, I get the impression that you might possibly value China even more than you do Japan. Four years ago, during the previous presidential election, it was reported—even by Japanese media outlets—that you ridiculed President Trump for not knowing that the Japanese Constitution was drafted by the U.S. after WWII. I got the feeling that, deep down inside, you want to keep Japan down. How do you actually view Japan? Do you see the country as even less important than China?

BIDEN'S G.S.

I would feel bad if your work (this recording) didn't get much of an audience, so let me do a little extra to help you out. You mentioned that I might think that China is more important than Japan and so on. But you want to know how I really feel. Well, I am a guardian spirit, so I will tell you how I really feel. I don't think I would say this if I was here in person, but I will say it now because I am a guardian spirit. My true feelings are that I don't mind if there's a war between the U.S. and China, but I want to limit the battlefield to at furthest Japan. I won't let the war come all the way to San Francisco. We will end the battlefield of the final war in Japan.

B
Even if you make Japan the battlefield, who do you think will ultimately win, China or the U.S.?

BIDEN'S G.S.
If it's a draw, we will have no choice but to divide Japan in half between China and the U.S.

B
Is this Biden's true intention?

BIDEN'S G.S.
I won't let the war come all the way to the U.S. I won't let it come all the way to Hawaii. They have nuclear weapons

too, so both sides are scared of it developing into an all-out war. So, I'm sure that we would come to an agreement at some point before that.

His awareness of the science and technology competition with China

A
But that's assuming you have balanced military power, right? The U.S. is stronger at the moment, but you will be surpassed at some point.

BIDEN'S G.S.
Hmm...

A
The reason that President Trump seems so nervous about 5G is that it will completely change the future military structure of the world. If China were to capture and gain total control over it, then the U.S. would have no hope of winning. Then, there will be a day that even you will be occupied.

BIDEN'S G.S.

I don't know what will come of it once I get elected, but the current administration is now beginning to focus on strengthening its Space Force. The reason the U.S. Space Force exists is to find ways to deter attacks from Chinese satellites as well as attacks that could destroy the U.S. satellites. People are actually working on this right now. The military is working in tandem with Houston, so the work itself will likely go ahead whether I get elected or not.

The U.S. is well aware of the fact that things like electromagnetic pulse attacks from space would render all kinds of equipment non-functional, so that's why. I think the reason that the U.S. is trying to make sure that most Chinese products are used in only China and not in other countries is so that if China is the only place that uses the Chinese version of TikTok and things like that for example, then we will be able to come up with attacks that destroy only the functions of those products.

A

President Trump is also taking a hardline stance toward Huawei. Do you plan to be tough on them as well?

BIDEN'S G.S.

Well, I wouldn't be able to stop that on my own anyway. The defensive technologies for that are progressing on their own, including in both the private sector and academia. So, what Trump is doing, hmm... If we share (with Huawei), then both (defensive technologies and private sector) will be destroyed.

China is expanding its military for defensive purpose

A

However, the biggest difference between you and China is that you are trying to profit individuals as well as in general through trade. But China conducts trade in order to ultimately pour all of its profits into its military. When China comes across intellectual properties and technologies that can be repurposed for military use, it pours all of them into its military.

After all, their purpose is to outstrip the U.S. and gain dominance.

BIDEN'S G.S.

No, that would be impossible.

A

You might think it's impossible, but the differences in military power between the U.S. and China will eventually shrink.

BIDEN'S G.S.

No, that's...

A

You may think it's impossible, but President Trump doesn't.

BIDEN'S G.S.

Listen. That would be impossible. China may be expanding its military, but right now, it's for defensive purposes. So...

A

So, you think that China is doing it for defense?

BIDEN'S G.S.

Right now, there is a huge difference in military power between China and the U.S., so if they don't get stronger, they won't be able to defend themselves.

President Trump is now trying to crush China's ambition of becoming no. 1 in the world in 2040

A

Right now, they are just biding their time.

BIDEN'S G.S.

Yeah, right, that's why...

A

However, they intend to reverse this situation within the next 10 to 20 years.

BIDEN'S G.S.

But Trump is trying to start it earlier. China is considering starting military conflict once their economy surpasses that of the U.S. And at that point, the U.S. will be at a slight disadvantage, so Trump is trying to start it first. In other words, from 2040... although predictions are never accurate, one prediction is that China will have the world's strongest economy, and the U.S. will be surpassed from 2040. Now, that is 20 years in the future, so I don't exactly know, but at that time, China will be starting to achieve military superiority. So, I think that Trump's plan is to crush China's military ambitions now in 2020, 20 years in advance.

A
What about you?

BIDEN'S G.S.
I don't believe that China will ever surpass the U.S.

A
You don't think they will be able to. What's your reason to say that?

BIDEN'S G.S.
The reason why is... hmm. As you can see from China now stealing all kinds of intellectual properties, I base it on the fact that, fundamentally, pirated goods are pirated and can never beat the real thing, whether they are watches, jewelry, or whatever.

He leaks his true feelings about Japan, Taiwan, and Hong Kong

C

I would like to ask you a little more about your true feelings. I was thinking about the true intentions behind your earlier comment about wanting to limit the battlefield to no further than Japan. To me as a Japanese person, it sounded like you see Japan as an object of profit to be shared between the U.S. and China, or sacrificing Japan is completely fine.

BIDEN'S G.S.

No, I have no intention of sacrificing Japan any time soon. There are other places I would before sacrificing Japan. Taiwan will become a battlefield before Japan does, so it might end in Taiwan. Or it might end in Hong Kong before it ever gets to Taiwan. There may be some sacrifices made in Hong Kong.

C

The Japan-U.S. alliance is extremely important to Japanese people. Do you not think of Japan as an ally? Or do you not consider Japan to be important?

BIDEN'S G.S.

No, that's not the case at all. I am probably much more of a friend to you than Trump is. Trump says that, in terms of military costs, the Japan-U.S. Security Treaty isn't worth it all and that it won't work if the U.S. is not protected and the U.S. is paying only to protect Japan alone. He says that Japan should bear more of the costs. The idea is that you should protect your own country on your own. But Japan doesn't want to protect itself. And that's why the U.S. is doing more than it should for so long. Trump is a businessman, so I think that if he sees it as a deficit from a business point of view, then he can even sever the alliance. That's the kind of person he is. He's the kind of person that decides out of the blue to build a wall along the border with Mexico.

He may even stir up commotion by demanding Japan to pay four times or even 10 times as much *Omoiyari Yosan* (sympathy budget), and declaring that, if Japan refuses, then the U.S. won't step in if Japan gets attacked. And he may enjoy it because he's good at stirring up a commotion. And Japan will pay up immediately, otherwise it's the equivalent of giving China permission to pounce on Japan like a wolf.

C

So, when you say that you are a friend to Japan, do you mean in your heart that Japan is under the protection of the U.S. military and that you want the occupation system to continue as it is?

BIDEN'S G.S.

Yes. There are some types of aeronautical and space-related technologies that the U.S. doesn't permit Japan to have. After all, when Japan bears its fangs, it's pretty scary too. Japan has gone up against countries 10 times its size. That's why I want to maintain Japan as a buffer zone.

A

How do you feel about President Truman for having dropped atomic bombs on Japan? Was he right to do that? Was it meaningful?

BIDEN'S G.S.

Hmm. You ask penetrating questions, don't you? We should have decided to speak English today. Hmm…

B

You idealize a world without nuclear weapons, but, as a U.S. statesman yourself, what are your views on the dropping of atomic bombs on Japan?

BIDEN'S G.S.

Well, I feel the same as President Obama, "Death fell from the sky."

B

So, the U.S. bears no responsibility?

A

I'm going to avoid commenting further.

Asking about Biden's health problems

A

We are almost out of time, but I have a few more things to ask. Some people have expressed concerns that you may be suffering from dementia. You make quite a few mistakes when speaking...

BIDEN'S G.S.

That's not racial discrimination but, how do I say, human discrimination.

B

Some people are worried about your health, but how is your health in actuality? Are you confident that you will be able to endure the coming four-year term, and maybe even eight years if you get a second term?

A

How do you see it from the perspective of a guardian spirit?

BIDEN'S G.S.

Well, many of my family members have died, and I too have lived through various misfortunes, so I know what it's like. Even Franklin Roosevelt, who was in a wheelchair while he was president, survived the Great Depression and through the war...

A

I think Roosevelt was pretty clear-headed, though. You (Mr. Biden) forget words, and you seem to sometimes forget whether you are running in a presidential election or senatorial election. Also, you postponed your debate with President Trump, right? Will you be having the debate?

BIDEN'S G.S.

Well, my personality isn't as unpleasant as Trump's, so...

A

Is it true that you are scared of having a live debate?

BIDEN'S G.S.

He launches personal attacks without hesitation, right? When he heard that my vice-presidential running mate is a Black woman, he said that I had selected the worst possible person.

A

Well, I understand that. So, are your intentions, as his guardian spirit, being directly conveyed to Mr. Biden himself on Earth?

BIDEN'S G.S.

I don't know. I can't tell.

A

Are there times that you feel things aren't going well? Like the actual Mr. Biden on Earth is saying strange things. Does anything like that happen?

BIDEN'S G.S.

Well, whether I guard him or not, I don't think it would affect the outcome.

A

It wouldn't affect the outcome.

BIDEN'S G.S.

No, not by much.

A

I see.

4

Discovering the True Nature of Biden's Soul

His previous life was as a sheriff in the old west, and two-lives ago was as a slave trader

A

May we ask you about your past lives?

B

In regard to you, the guardian spirit who is here today, when did you live on Earth, and who were you?

BIDEN'S G.S.

Hmm... Hmm... [*About five seconds of silence.*] Hmm...

B

Were you American?

BIDEN'S G.S.

I get the feeling that I was in the old west.

A

The period of western expansion in the U.S.?

B

Were you white?

BIDEN'S G.S.

Yes, yes, that's right. And at the time, I felt very bad about taking land from Native Americans. But then, that's what enabled us to make it all the way to the west coast. From the point of view of the Native Americans, though, it was definitely an invasion. People, mainly from Britain, took land from the Native Americans and forced them onto reservations. And they spread American prosperity all the way to the west coast. To them, it was to put America First. But poor Native Americans. Even though they were the original owners, they became a minority and were driven back. I was there during the old west, and it was exciting that the U.S. extended all the way to the Pacific Ocean, but there were some unfortunate aspects to it as well. In that sense, I am aware that there are tragic happenings with racial discrimination.

At the time, what was I doing? Well, I was helping to pioneer the west... Hmm... As a sheriff maybe. I get the feeling that I was a sheriff. I feel like I wore a badge and worked as a sheriff.

A

Does that mean that you shot a bunch of Native Americans?

BIDEN'S G.S.

Hmm... Yeah, that happened. I didn't only shoot Native Americans, though. I also had to maintain law and order in town. There were also many Black slaves.

A

Have you ever had any connection with Mr. Obama in any of your reincarnations?

BIDEN'S G.S.

Mr. Obama... [*About 10 seconds of silence.*] Hmm... [*About 10 seconds of silence.*] Mr. Obama... It may have been one life earlier. But I get the feeling that I brought someone from Africa as a slave. It probably wasn't Mr. Obama himself (his past life), though. It was a relative of his.

A

Do you mean that you were a slave trader?

BIDEN'S G.S.

Yeah, I was. I think it was around two lives ago. Probably.

A

Two lives ago.

In a past life, he was a Jesuit missionary preaching in China

B

Can you recall any reincarnations prior to that?

A

Did you ever have any connection with China or Japan? Or anywhere in the East?

BIDEN'S G.S.

[*Breathes out.*] Prior to that... Prior to that... I somewhat get the feeling that I had gone to China as a missionary. Hmm.

A

A missionary.

BIDEN'S G.S.

A Christian missionary.

A

Around when?

B

Which era of Chinese history?

A

Was it during the Opium War?

BIDEN'S G.S.

No, it was a little further back than that.

A

Further back? Portugal was...

BIDEN'S G.S.

Yeah. And Japan...

C

Was it during the Qing dynasty?

BIDEN'S G.S.

Hmm? Christian missionaries also came to Japan at that time, so it was probably even further back than the Qing dynasty.

A

Oh, around that period. Were you a Jesuit missionary?

BIDEN'S G.S.

Yeah, yeah. That's right. So, I was probably from Spain or someplace like that.

A

Were you in the Jesuit Order?

BIDEN'S G.S.

Yes. ...I think so.

A

What were you doing at the time?

BIDEN'S G.S.

I was a missionary.

A

As a missionary, what were you doing in regard to Asia?

BIDEN'S G.S.

Hmm. For missionary work. I had come to spread the Gospel.

B

So, you are basically a Christian soul…

C

Was it around the time of Japan's Warring States period?

BIDEN'S G.S.

Also, trading groups had come with me. Missionary work and trade were a set. Because missionary work, trade, and the military functioned in tandem.

A

In a past life, Mr. Xi Jinping is said to have been Genghis Khan during the Yuan dynasty. Did you have any connection with him anywhere in Asia or the West around that time?

BIDEN'S G.S.

Genghis Khan... [*About 10 seconds of silence.*] Isn't he the one who brought the Plague to Europe?

A

Yes, that's right.

BIDEN'S G.S.

Right? And he's doing the same thing now. He's the one who brought the Plague. ...that's the feeling I get. It was terrible. Things were terrible in Europe then, right?

A

Were you in Europe?

BIDEN'S G.S.

Hmm. ...yes. I don't really know, but anyway, I get the feeling that people were living a nightmare.

A

You feel like it was a nightmare.

BIDEN'S G.S.

Yeah, yeah, yeah.

Who guides Biden's guardian spirit?

B

In the spiritual world, what kind of realm do you live in now?

BIDEN'S G.S.
Hmm?

B

The spiritual world that you live in now, what kind of realm...

BIDEN'S G.S.
What kind of realm...

B

Or who are your friends that are near to you?

BIDEN'S G.S.
Hmm... Well, a long time ago... Right now, America is a great big country, it's great. But a long time ago, it was small. It was founded by people who fled from Britain. They

gradually developed it into a country, and they were also in competition with France. The Declaration of Independence was a little over 200 years ago. America has developed in the same way that companies usually grow—from a small company to a medium-sized, then a large company. And I think that you may say the wrong thing if you look back at it from the modern perspective. People like police chiefs and mayors may seem insignificant to you, but at the time, they had as much power as senators do now.

A

If you, a sheriff in a past life, become a president in this life, that would be quite a promotion.

BIDEN'S G.S.

No... they're not so different.

A

They're not different?

BIDEN'S G.S.

No. Anyways that's how things were.

A

Is there anyone who has done that (gone from a sheriff to president)?

BIDEN'S G.S.

Well, American democracy was just about a gathering of people from all walks of life having discussions and making decisions.

B

Is there anyone that guides or instructs you, the guardian spirit of Mr. Biden? Also, what kind of god do you believe in?

A

Right now, leading up to the presidential election...

BIDEN'S G.S.

No, I can't recognize any gods. But I was a missionary; I remember being a missionary, so hmm... I could be guided by the Christian God, or by some type of angelic beings that serve the Christian God. Yeah.

B

Have you ever heard the names "El Cantare" or "Thoth"?

BIDEN'S G.S.

Oh, that's a difficult question.

B

It's difficult?

BIDEN'S G.S.

Yeah, it's difficult.

A

Do you have any connection with Francis Xavier?

BIDEN'S G.S.

Xavier... There were many people with the name Xavier.

A

Oh, so you don't know.

BIDEN'S G.S.

No, I don't know.

A

I see.

He protests the nickname "Sleepy Joe"

A

Well, it's nearly time to end this session...

BIDEN'S G.S.

Oh, OK.

A

Any last...

BIDEN'S G.S.

[*To C.*] Do you have anything you would like to say on "Trump's behalf"?

C

President Trump has given you the nickname "Sleepy Joe." Do you have any comments about that? I understand that it gives the impression that you are foolish and slow-witted.

BIDEN'S G.S.

Well, I will be 78 years old this November, so... But Trump needs to be told, "Hey, if you do another term, you'll be 78 years old by then too."

B

In conclusion, do you have a message you would like to convey to people in the U.S., Japan, and the world?

BIDEN'S G.S.

Hmm. If I am elected president, the world will become peaceful. If Trump remains president, he will be in a hurry to rack up achievements, and the world will be dotted with wars. Conflicts and racial strife will expand in scope, and international organizations will rattle and crumble. The world will likely once again end up as a mosaic (be fractured into numerous tiny factions). So, I would like the entire world to work to ensure that people vote for Biden without hesitation.

B

OK.

5

Asking His Views on the Novel Coronavirus That Originated in China

He wants to hold President Trump more responsible for the coronavirus problem than China

D

Excuse me, but can I ask just one thing here at the end?

BIDEN'S G.S.

Uh-huh.

D

Earlier, you mentioned that Genghis Khan was the one who brought the Plague and that he is doing it again right now.

BIDEN'S G.S.

Hmm.

D

The coronavirus is now spreading rampantly in the U.S. In regard to the coronavirus issue, what connection do you think it has with China?

BIDEN'S G.S.

Hmm...

B

Mr. Trump claims that it originated in China...

D

I think the reason that Mr. Trump is being so strict with China right now is that he is taking a hardline approach, even going so far as to claim that China intentionally spread the coronavirus in the U.S.

BIDEN'S G.S.

Hmm, well...

D

What are your personal views on the coronavirus?

BIDEN'S G.S.

Well, that is, hmm, according to the information I have received, China and the U.S. had been jointly developing the virus. And I heard that the U.S. pulled out because China began to use the virus militarily in actual combat. Lots of Chinese people came to the U.S., and I think that the researchers involved may have done something. But I don't want to aggravate the situation too much. So, until we get some clear evidence, instead of attacking China for infecting the U.S. with the virus, I would rather focus on holding Trump responsible for refusing to wear a mask and for further spreading infections by overly prioritizing the economy.

D

So far, millions of Americans—your people—have died. That's...

BIDEN'S G.S.

No, they haven't. Not millions. Well over 100,000 have died.

D

Ah, the number of the infected is in the millions.

BIDEN'S G.S.

The number of infected people has exceeded five million.

D

And that will keep increasing, right?

BIDEN'S G.S.

Hmm, you have dementia, don't you?

D

Are you saying that you don't need to do anything about it?

BIDEN'S G.S.

Well, pharmaceutical companies are developing a vaccine right now. So I'm sure it will be made in the near future. A vaccine will be completed during my first term in office. Nothing can be done until then, though, so please go ahead and get infected. Then, once we have the vaccine, you will be cured.

He intends to withdraw the nuclear weapons on U.S. military bases in Asia to Guam and Hawaii

D

One more thing. I don't believe you answered the question about nuclear weapons. You mentioned that you take after Mr. Obama, but he's the kind of person who claps upon watching a video showing the atomic bombs being dropped on Japan. What do you actually think about nuclear weapons?

BIDEN'S G.S.

Hmm... I am sure that everyone knows that the U.S. military bases in Vietnam (Author's Note: The guardian spirit of Biden is believed to have mistakenly said Vietnam instead of Okinawa.) and on mainland Japan have nuclear weapons. I intend to withdraw those to Guam and Hawaii. I want to make sure "Japan has no nuclear weapons" to avoid giving China or North Korea the excuse to attack Japan with nuclear weapons.

A

Really? I see.

Well, let's finish here today.

BIDEN'S G.S.

Oh, I used up a lot of the time scheduled for Trump's (guardian spirit) interview [*laughs*].

So, can I go now?

A

Yes. Thank you very much.

B

Thank you very much.

BIDEN'S G.S.

Thank you.

RYUHO OKAWA

[*Claps twice.*] OK. Thank you.

Spiritual Interview with the Guardian Spirit of Donald Trump

Originally recorded in Japanese on August 17, 2020,
in the Special Lecture Hall of Happy Science in Japan,
and later translated into English.

Donald Trump (1946 - Present)

An American politician and businessman. The 45th president of the United States. Republican. Born in New York City. After graduating from the University of Pennsylvania in 1968, he worked at a real estate company that his father was running and became its president in 1971. In 1983, he built the Trump Tower, known as the "world's most luxurious building" on Fifth Avenue in New York. He succeeded in real estate development and hotel and casino management. On January 20, 2017, he was inaugurated as the 45th president of the U.S.

1

President Trump's Chances of Being Reelected

Interview with Biden's guardian spirit should just be an appendix

RYUHO OKAWA

Now let's move onto a spiritual interview with the guardian spirit of President Donald Trump. We would like to ask about his current thoughts regarding his reelection campaign and his opinion about world affairs.

[*While clapping slowly and softly.*] Guardian spirit of President Donald Trump.

DONALD TRUMP'S GUARDIAN SPIRIT
Uhh... Hmm...

A
Good morning.

TRUMP'S G.S.
Yes.

A

Thank you for coming today.

TRUMP'S G.S.

Hmm.

A

You haven't been coming to Happy Science for the last few months.

TRUMP'S G.S.

Busy. I've been busy.

A

Despite your great exertion and efforts for the world, the U.S. media is trying to portray you as a villain. Yet, you have maintained your hard-line policy against China without losing your way. I think you will become a central figure in the future creation of world peace. Earlier, we summoned Mr. Biden's guardian spirit.

TRUMP'S G.S.

Ah, Biden. That (spiritual interview) was meaningless. Pointless. I think you should just delete it.

A

[*Laughs.*]

TRUMP'S G.S.

Yes. If you decide to publish it as a book, you should summarize what he just said in one hour and five minutes in five pages and put it in as an appendix. The rest can all be my spiritual message.

The media attacks President Trump because he's powerful

A

I think Mr. Biden's spiritual interview was valuable in that he exposed his secrets. The U.S. media doesn't cover anything bad about Mr. Biden, like corruption.

TRUMP'S G.S.

Because otherwise, he'll lose. If they report his weaknesses, we'd all be sorry for him.

A

They don't report that, and instead, they're bashing Mr. Trump.

TRUMP'S G.S.

Because he's going to lose. He'll lose.

A

Right.

TRUMP'S G.S.

Yes. If they report all his weaknesses, the media will become the bad guy. They attack powerful people because that's how they justify what they do.

A

But the media doesn't care about good and evil.

TRUMP'S G.S.

No. They're attacking me because they know I'm stronger.

A

Yes, that's true. Which is why, at the beginning of this year, your chances of reelection were really high.

TRUMP'S G.S.

Of course. I'll be in it for another five years or so. If I'm not—Look around the world. There are people like Putin, who's been president for decades, Xi Jinping, who's in it for life, and Mr. Abe, who's serving as if he is prime minister for life too. So, the world... And Merkel doesn't step down. Everyone's trying really hard.

American power will decline when our negotiation abilities decline.

A

Yes, I agree.

TRUMP'S G.S.

So, it's not so easy.

Trumponomics and *Trump-Keizai-Kakumei* can save Japan

A

Today, we would like you to clarify everything you want to promote ahead of the election, which the U.S. media doesn't cover properly: everything that the Americans,

Japanese and other people around the world should know about.

TRUMP'S G.S.

You know, if I had absolute power—I wish I had the authority to choose Japan's politicians and officers. I would appoint Mr. C, who translated *Trumponomics*[*] into Japanese, as state minister for reviving the economy.

A

Yes, I agree.

TRUMP'S G.S.

So what if he's a non-government worker, it doesn't matter. I think it's OK if up to half of your ministers are people from the private sector. It's OK if he doesn't have a seat in the Diet. Just take a copy of *Trumponomics*, and that other recent book. What was it?

A

Trump-Keizai-Kakumei[†].

---

[*] See p.28.

[†] Stephen Moore, and Arthur B Laffer, *Trump-Keizai-Kakumei* (literally, "Trump's Economic Revolution") trans. Motohisa Fujii (Tokyo: IRH Press, 2020).

TRUMP'S G.S.

Trump-Keizai-Kakumei. Take those two books and walk into the prime minister's office with your authority as the person in charge of economic revival, and get them to do what's in those books. Then Japan is as good as saved. It wouldn't matter who's the prime minister. As long as you do that, you'll only be left with small issues.

Biden will lose because his economic policy is bad

A

[*To C*] Do you have any questions regarding the economy?

C

Yes. As news reports say, Mr. Biden is pushing for a tax raise. In other words, he's trying to completely reverse everything Mr. Trump has done. The media is sending out the message that Mr. Trump is clearly at a disadvantage. What are your actual chances of victory?

TRUMP'S G.S.

Well, I cut corporate tax rate down to 21 percent, but Mr. Biden vows that if he becomes president, he'll raise it to 28 percent or something. So, taxes will rise for businesses. If you do that at a time of economic crisis, like now, there'll be more unemployment. Basically, businesses would have to fire their workers, and streamline everything. A lot of places will go bankrupt.

Biden is aiming for big government. He wants more tax revenue. He wants more tax revenue and injects money into those failing businesses. He wants to do what Japan is doing. In that sense, he's way behind Japan, and he's trying to copy them. He's hopeless. He'll lose. People who do the wrong thing lose.

2

The Course for Containing Dictatorial China

Hong Kong's chief executive may not live to see the New Year

C

In addition to the American economy, what is of deep international concern is the Hong Kong crisis. Mr. Trump recently spoke against the arrests of Hong Kong's democratic activists. You might not be able to tell us exactly what you're planning, but do you have something in mind?

TRUMP'S G.S.

Yes, I do. We also have information about Hong Kong's chief executive and her aides: who they are, where they live, their patterns of behavior; we know it all. We've already simulated a strike. We're really good at accurate pinpoint strikes, and we might have to do one. We can't target Beijing, because it'll turn into a war, but what I can say is that Hong Kong's chief executive may not live to see the New Year.

C

Mr. Biden's guardian spirit doesn't seem to mind turning Japan into a battlefield. What are your thoughts on that?

TRUMP'S G.S.

[*Laughs.*] Ridiculous. He's saying whatever, because the Japanese people can't vote in the presidential election. No, that must not happen. I'll destroy the enemy before Japan turns into a battlefield. Of course, I will. What else is the alliance for?

"I can use a fleet of five nations, but Biden can't use the British army"

B

A member of Trump's Cabinet visited Taiwan recently.

TRUMP'S G.S.

Yes.

B

What are you planning in terms of Taiwan relations?

TRUMP'S G.S.

We'll take Taiwan, and Japan, and also India, to establish a "contain China" network. Luckily, Russia's Putin is also pro-Trump so we don't have to strike them. Russia has promised that they won't become our enemy, which makes it possible to contain China.

With India, I want to sell them American weapons and tell them to create combat forces on the same level as the U.S. military. We've already sold weapons to Taiwan, and quite a bit to Japan too. But well, there's a problem with Japan's leaders.

So, at least these three countries and the U.S. military moving independently will establish a "fleet of four nations". Then Britain will probably join us.

But if Biden becomes president, Britain won't cooperate because Biden's against Brexit. He's saying, "Go back. Get back into the EU!"

Biden is of Irish descent if you go way back. He was just saying he belongs to the American elite or something, but that's a lie. [*laughs*] He's of Irish descent. It's a difficult issue because Brexit could put Northern Ireland at a disadvantage. Northern Ireland would be divided in their choice whether to go with the rest of the U.K., or to go with the EU. That's why he doesn't want Brexit.

The U.K. is saying they'll give three million Hong Kong citizens the chance to apply for British citizenship: a visa plan. But if Biden becomes president, this plan will become unprotected. The U.K. won't join us if it's unprotected. If I'm president, they will.

So, like I just said, my plan is to get the military power of at least Japan, Taiwan, India, the mainland U.S.– the U.S. military – and the British Army, and put pressure on China.

What it means to normalize diplomatic relations between Israel and the UAE

A

After you sent a Cabinet member to Taiwan, people are now thinking that next comes diplomatic recognition. You did the same thing with the UAE when they recently normalized relations with Israel.

TRUMP'S G.S.

That was a good move, right?

A

Yes.

TRUMP'S G.S.

You weren't expecting it, were you?

B

The timing came as a surprise.

TRUMP'S G.S.

Yeah, I'm pretty good at these things. With the Israel-Arab conflict, you know, people think I'm trying to destroy Islam, but there are Muslims in America too. That's not what I'm trying to do.

I'm showing them that I don't have religious prejudices, and by connecting the Arab side with Israel, I want people to understand that my support for Israel doesn't mean I want to destroy Islam.

"I want to turn Iran into a democracy and stabilize the Middle East"

TRUMP'S G.S.

We made a strike on Iraq in the past, but Iran has a problem in their political system too. Their media is censored, which is the same as China. Economic inflation has caused lots of riots and many, many people have been arrested.

There is truth in what the people are saying. Muslims are rioting against the government led by the supreme leader of Islam. For a country that prides itself in solidarity, this just can't be happening. That's why they won't cover it in the news.

If they have even a bit of democracy in them, they need to accept the fact that the Muslims are rioting against the government led by the supreme leader of Islam, saying it is horrible. They need to reform. But they don't listen, because they have obstinate minds.

But they have an inflated sense of pride in the fact that they have 6,000 years of history, whereas America only has 200. They're boasting, "You became a country only 200 years ago, but we were a country 6,000 years ago." We need to shake them up a bit. I don't want to have a full-blown war, but we need to change them into a democracy.

You know, it might look like a two-front war, but Iran has less than a tenth of the power of the U.S. We only need to spare a little effort on them. Anyhow, I want to stabilize the Middle East.

On President Trump's North Korea diplomacy

TRUMP'S G.S.

They're trying to create another "axis of evil" with Iran, China, North Korea, and Russia. But Russia is half-hearted. And with North Korea, I met with Kim Jong-un and defanged him, so he won't fully resist when I say something.

A

So, you gradually won the support of those surrounding countries and now you are targeting China.

TRUMP'S G.S.

Yes, yes, yes. People may think I failed in my diplomacy with North Korea, but by meeting him many times and praising him and so on, I made it so that even if a war broke out between China and the U.S...

China originally wanted to use North Korea. They wanted to turn North Korea into an outpost and make them fight against Japan and Taiwan as a scapegoat. But now it's really hard for China to do that. North Korea is not going to listen to China.

China wants to strike down the American economy

C

I would like to ask about COVID-19. You, Mr. Trump's guardian spirit, haven't been coming to Happy Science recently, so we haven't heard your thoughts on the coronavirus pandemic. A noteworthy point is that President Trump has been calling it the "China Virus," which has become a target for the leftist media. Can you please tell us your thoughts on where it originated, the intention behind it, and what exactly is happening?

TRUMP'S G.S.

I think it was created with the purpose of fighting a virus war. The virus is spreading in the U.S. but, as Biden said, we're putting a lot of effort into making a vaccine. We can't stop it without a vaccine.

If we make a vaccine and it goes around, then, to an extent, we'll be able to deal with the virus. Until then, I think it's more important to stop the American economy from slowing down.

So, the virus might spread. It might look like it's spreading, but I'm more afraid of an economic slowdown. We might succeed in making a vaccine that can cure the ill people, but if the economy experiences a major slowdown, it will never go back to normal.

China's strategy is to strike down the American economy and become the world's number one power. That's definitely it. And for some reason, there have been no additional COVID cases or deaths in China since March.

It's too much of a miracle to be true [*laughs*]. I can't understand how such a miracle can happen in a country that doesn't believe in God. I think Xi Jinping is trying to become a living god.

A
So, the general outline is clear.

TRUMP'S G.S.

The virus stopped when Xi went to Wuhan, right? It stopped spreading, right? That's it. That's socialism right there.

A

Inside sources have leaked that the numbers are too low to be true.

TRUMP'S G.S.

It's impossible [*laughs*].

B

They just stopped counting the number of cases.

TRUMP'S G.S.

That's right. They stopped doing tests.

B

One source indicates that hospitals are beyond their capacity, so when COVID patients are carried in, they're rejected and considered dead. They are burned and the remains are buried.

TRUMP'S G.S.

Yes. The hospitals can't cope with it. Their logic is, "don't do tests, and no one is infected."

B

I've heard that people who can't go to hospital die at home.

TRUMP'S G.S.

Yes. Lots of them are poor people. It's spreading.

We'll keep Japan and Taiwan's damages to a minimum

A

A virologist formerly employed at the University of Hong Kong has defected to the U.S. and exposed the truth. Do you intend to make a decisive strike against China after you expose one or two other pieces of evidence?

TRUMP'S G.S.

Well, I might get in trouble if I speak about this.

A

So it's a secret that you can't tell yet?

TRUMP'S G.S.

A strike doesn't become a noble cause unless it's retaliation for severe damages. The damages need to go beyond a certain point. It's hard for me to say this as president because it will anger the Americans, but...

A

Oh... that's... OK.

TRUMP'S G.S.

How big the damages... Well, we've done simulations and calculations on how big the damage has to be for the global community to say "the U.S. is doing the right thing" when we deploy our military in a fit of rage.

A

Right. Do you have any conclusive evidence?

TRUMP'S G.S.

Pretty much.

A

You have it?

TRUMP'S G.S.

Yes. We know everything from the elementary stages 15 years ago when they started tweaking with the bat virus. We pretty much know everything.

But we need to think about what would happen if it becomes a military matter, and what we need to do after it. We need to be careful because there's a possibility that our ally Japan will incur economic and military damages. We're simulating how to keep them to a minimum.

Also, Taiwan's very close to China geographically. We can't do something that might end up reducing the population of Taiwan to one-third. They only have a population of around 23 million, so if China tries, they can probably reduce the population down to half, or even one-third. We can't let that happen.

"I will be reelected and bring about Xi Jinping's downfall within two years"

TRUMP'S G.S.

But I'm not a militarist. The first thing for me is to be reelected and to bring about Xi Jinping's downfall within two years. That is the first.

A

I see.

TRUMP'S G.S.

That's what I'll choose to do. I think it's a peaceful approach, you know. There's a lot of pent-up discontent within China at the moment. There are people who seek for Xi's downfall.

The officials want to hide the poor numbers and other bad evidence from getting out: unfavorable economic statistics and unfavorable statistics on COVID cases and deaths. But there are many people inside China who are burning with righteous indignation. There'll be lots of leaks, and political leaders who revolt. I want to support those people, of course.

A

This happened at a recent public ceremony. Xi Jinping was introduced to the audience, after whom Premier Li Keqiang was introduced. But just as he stood up to address the people, the next person was immediately introduced, thus publically humiliating Li. The scene is streaming on the internet. They are clearly denouncing Li Keqiang.

TRUMP'S G.S.

Yes, they are.

A

What are your thoughts on this internal struggle?

TRUMP'S G.S.

Well, if you're the chairman with a premier under you, and everyone thinks that the premier is better than you, and there's a lot of discontent among the public, it is a very dangerous political situation, isn't it?

Li Keqiang was bright enough to study at Harvard, but he gave up studying there and stayed in China because in China, people who study abroad in the U.S. are treated as second-class. But he's someone who could have studied at

Harvard, meaning that he admires the U.S. and he has been studying about the U.S. He keeps those two sides separate.

On one side, he's loyal to Xi Jinping, and on the other, he has his own opinion. If there is a coup d'état while he is still in power, he could climb the ladder. I think that's why Xi wants to shave off his power.

The basic strategy: cause an internal conflict among the central powers and divide their opinions

A
Are you setting up an internal split?

TRUMP'S G.S.
Setting up? Me?

A
Yes.

TRUMP'S G.S.
Setting up? Well, China's manipulating the statistics, and erasing unfavorable stats. That's why this year (2020)

they'll probably announce that they've made positive economic growth. They might keep the percentage low, but they will still say that they made a one to three percent growth. But people with a guilty conscience will start to say, "That's wrong."

The true growth rate will at best be negative 15 percent. It might be worse. But they'll manipulate it and publish a positive percentage. People with a conscience wouldn't be able to bear it. And that's why there will be an internal conflict.

So the basic strategy against countries that try to invade other outside countries is to encourage an internal power conflict, to divide their opinions.

We cannot fight China unless Trump is reelected as "wartime president"

A

The Chinese consulate in Houston was closed due to suspicions of spy activity. Do you have any other similar strategies?

TRUMP'S G.S.

Umm... It's a paradise for spies. They're doing it everywhere. But when we try to get spies into China, it's very difficult, because they're quite a closed country. It's a big country, but it's a closed country.

If the situation in Wuhan had all been disclosed since January, the world could have dealt with it faster.

And now those floods. Yangtze River and Yellow River have flooded, and there are said to be over 65 million people affected, with tens of billions of dollars in damages. I mean, we don't even know if this is true, but I'm sure the true figures can't be smaller than what they're saying.

If 65 million is true, I think close to 100 million people have had their homes washed away or their wellbeing threatened. The Chinese government probably doesn't have the ability to build temporary housing like they do in Japan. So, I'm sure there are many people out there who have nothing to eat and are living in virus-infected communities.

If this information gets out, the government will immediately be at risk. Right now, they're censoring the information, but there will be a point where some people will not be able to tolerate it anymore.

I also want to let more of the world know about the resistance in Hong Kong. And I want to create a revolt inside China.

But that needs time. So my reelection is imperative. Otherwise, it's August now, so we only have until October to fight. It's impossible to end it all within that time. Their cover-ups might last until around October, so I need more time.

A
Yes.

TRUMP'S G.S.
That's why I want Biden to step down.

A
[*Laughs.*] But the media is quite...

TRUMP'S G.S.
I'm a "wartime president". In fact, we have no time for an election. We shouldn't be doing one.

A
Yes, that's right.

TRUMP'S G.S.

That is said to be democracy's greatest weakness.

3

Prospects for the Presidential Election and China's Democratization

"If it looks like Biden will win, God will use His lightning of rage"

A

How does President Trump see the current odds?

TRUMP'S G.S.

The odds?

A

The media says that Biden has higher approval ratings.

TRUMP'S G.S.

Oh, that. Not a problem. I'll be reelected.

A

You'll win?

TRUMP'S G.S.

Yes. If it looks like I won't be reelected until the last moment, with Biden leading and likely to win, God will use His "lightning of rage."

A

Is that agreed upon?

TRUMP'S G.S.

It will all be over if Biden dies from a stroke or something, won't it?

A

Does Biden actually have dementia?

TRUMP'S G.S.

They say he has a problem with his cerebral circulation.

A

A problem. OK.

TRUMP'S G.S.

So if that pops, it might be over for him.

A

It's over.

TRUMP'S G.S.

I have a "signed deed" from space people saying, "If it looks like Trump won't win, we will do it."

A

Is that right?

TRUMP'S G.S.

It's a space being who you know. He says, "If worst comes to worst, we will use our electric shock and cause a heart attack or a stroke."

A

Did you get a message like that?

TRUMP'S G.S.

Yes, yes, yes. I did. Well, I'm sure I'll win.

A

Do you still have another card up your sleeve that will trigger it?

TRUMP'S G.S.

Yes, I do.

A

There's the problem with Biden and China getting close, or him stopping the Ukrainian prosecution from investigating. He must have gained enormous amounts of profit for his son's company. This scandal hasn't come up yet in the election campaign. Will you be using these cards anytime soon?

TRUMP'S G.S.

I'll use them if I can. But just like our "minister C" said*, it'll all end if we do a debate. If we do three public debates, he'll collapse from a stroke at some point.

B

You might knock him out in one round.

TRUMP'S G.S.

Right? He'll get a stroke, get carried into the hospital, and it'll be over, right?

---

* Mr. C mentioned in a publishing seminar of *Trump-Keizai-Kakumei* that Mr. Trump will claim a landslide victory in a debate session against Mr. Biden.

A

Biden's team is trying to avoid a debate by keeping him in the basement.

TRUMP'S G.S.

He can't win that way. Not the U.S. presidential election.

You see, I don't eat good food, but I'm still brawny. I have a physique that's sturdy enough to play Superman. Superman is about 6'3", 220lbs. I weigh more, but I stay healthy: I don't eat in luxury, I don't drink, I don't smoke, I don't drink coffee.

I still have a lot of vitality. I'm too busy for that, but I can still make children for another 10 years.

We've already simulated the Taiwan crisis

C

You called yourself a wartime president.

TRUMP'S G.S.

Yes, yes! That's right.

C

Ever since declaring a state of national emergency you've been telling the people that the U.S. is now a wartime government. According to information about the Spirit World uncovered at Happy Science, the First Emperor of Qin (Qin Shi Huang)* is saying that China may launch a simultaneous attack on Taiwan and Okinawa. There's a possibility that China will move first. What are your thoughts?

TRUMP'S G.S.

I think Taiwan is prepared enough. I think Tsai Ing-wen has been expecting China to make a move within a year ever since Lee Teng-hui died. I'm thinking of preparing something for that.

It'll probably be from Guam. I don't know if we'll use long-range strike bombers or missiles. I shouldn't be telling you this.

But if need be, at the latest... We've already simulated it. Say, if I sign an Executive Order at 8 pm, then by 3 am the next morning, you'll see a certain location in China engulfed in a sea of flames.

---

* See Part Two, Chapter One, "Shin-no-Shikoutei-no-Reigen" (literally, "Spiritual Messages from Qin Shi Huang") in Ryuho Okawa, *Koukai-Reigen Rojin-no-Negai: Chugoku-ni-Jiyuu-o* (literally, "Spiritual Messages from Lu Xun: Let There Be Freedom in China") (Tokyo: IRH Press, 2020).

China's military training in the South China Sea is a diversion

A

China is holding military drills in the South China Sea more frequently than before.

TRUMP'S G.S.

Well, it's actually a diversion. They're thinking of starting a war out there.

They don't want to fight in mainland China, so they're thinking of waging war in the ocean because that way they can reduce the risk of incurring damages. China doesn't mind if everyone at their naval bases is slaughtered.

The troops stationed at the Spratly Islands would be mortified to hear it, but China plans to leave them there to die. The government would be happy if it works to keep the U.S. military occupied.

A

So I guess you're going to use that against them.

"There is no way China can attack Japan's U.S. military bases first"

C

I'm thinking about what could happen to Japan.

If the U.S. and China engage in a war, there is a chance that China will first target the U.S. military bases in Japan. Do you see this happening?

TRUMP'S G.S.

There is no way they can attack U.S. military bases first because we'll know before they enter into attack mode. We're way ahead of them in this kind of technology. If they go into attack mode, we'll immediately strike them down. We'll never fall behind them. We've already set up a wartime structure. It's going to be OK.

C

Does that mean you're planning everything under the assumption that the U.S. military will make a sweeping victory?

TRUMP'S G.S.

I mean [*laughs*], it'll be settled in one day. In one day, the world...

If the devil's minions at CNN ever decide to broadcast the footage, everyone will know what is happening. I'll try to make them see what's happening.

A

If you tell this to Japan, it will be chaos.

TRUMP'S G.S.

Yes, that's why I'll only tell Mr. Abe at the last moment. Otherwise, I won't say anything, because China can access all the information that Japan has.

A

Yes, I agree.

Right now, they're holding the Beidaihe meeting (summer summit) in China, and it is said to end in late August. There are rumors that this might be when they will think about conducting a military strike. I'm sure you can't tell us, but...

TRUMP'S G.S.

You know, I haven't been coming to Happy Science because I'm talkative, and I'll end up telling you everything.

A

China's very weak against the U.S., right? For example, they're very weak against Secretary of State Mike Pompeo whenever he criticizes them. It looks like China's main strategy is to wait until President Trump loses in the presidential election.

TRUMP'S G.S.

I'm sure they'll try to see how we'll respond. They'll be doing lots of suspicious activities around the South China Sea. And they'll probably do tricks like sending a thousand fishing vessels to the seas around the Senkaku Islands to see how Japan reacts, and how the U.S. reacts.

Japan's ultimate weapon against the CCP

A

Do you know about Master Ryuho Okawa's dream[*]? It's written in the book *Koukai-Reigen Rojin-no Negai*: a giant dragon with 17 heads threatens Japan, and Master Okawa uses his spiritual powers to slice it in two. The dragon is said to be the First Emperor of Qin (Qin Shi Huang). What do you think about this dream interpretation?

TRUMP'S G.S.

Well, Master Ryuho Okawa is Japan's ultimate weapon, isn't he? So ultimately, you don't need the Self-Defense Forces.

A

Oh, that's what... [*laughs*]

TRUMP'S G.S.

He can just use the power of prayer to kill Xi Jinping. I'm sure he can. That's what the dream means. I think it means that Master Okawa can slice Qin Shi Huang in two, but

---

[*] See the Afterword in Ryuho Okawa, *Shiva-Shin-no-Me-kara-Mita-Chikyuu-no-Mirai-Keikaku* (literally, "Future Plan of the Earth in the Eyes of God Shiva") and aforementioned *Koukai-Reigen Rojin-no-Negai* (both Tokyo: IRH Press, 2020).

he can also kill Xi Jinping with a curse. That's why he's the ultimate weapon. And no one will know.

China's post-Xi democratization

B

Earlier you revealed to us the strategy that you will bring down Xi Jinping within the next two years. What do you see happening in China after that?

TRUMP'S G.S.

I think it will be similar to Japan's Meiji Restoration, or the postwar period. We need to get them to make democratic reforms. We need to at least take those places that have turned into Auschwitz and open the lid, so to speak. Investigate them and disclose the information to the international community.

We need to disclose information on Uyghur, Southern Mongolia, and Tibet. And also what's happening in Hong Kong. Then we need a puppet ruler to head the reforms in China while being watched by the international community. I think that's what we need to do.

We're doing our research, but it's a very difficult country to grasp. We're starting to narrow down the strategies that we might be able to use.

Another way would be to take Chinese people living in the U.S. and send them back to China to contribute to the creation of a new government.

Stay still before you attack

A

I'd like to go back a little. You didn't come here during the most intense period when there were the virus outbreak and further complications in the U.S.-China relations. On the other hand, spirits such as Qin Shi Huang and Xi Jinping's guardian spirit came to Master Okawa when they lost composure.

TRUMP'S G.S.

[*Laughs.*] They all come from China. Yes.

A

It implies that you never lost your composure. How were you able to keep your peace of mind? Or was it because you didn't want to spill your secrets?

TRUMP'S G.S.

You know, when a leopard hunts an antelope, they approach very discreetly until they reach a distance close enough to win the chase. If they make a noise and scare the birds, it'll give the antelope away. It's the instinct of a beast of prey to approach softly. This is important.

A

If you thought you would lose in the election, you would lose your peace of mind, wouldn't you?

TRUMP'S G.S.

Oh, I will not lose. It will not happen.

A

No?

TRUMP'S G.S.

No way. I will shoot a missile into the Japanese Prime Minister's Official Residence before I do. I would tell them, "Show more support! Yell and shout, 'China is doing bad things! We need Trump, otherwise, we cannot protect Japan!'" I can put the pressure on them to say that if there is a chance that I might lose.

All it takes is a drone to fly there from the American base in Yokosuka and drop a dummy bomb to scare them. It is not like I cannot do it.

Mail-in ballots could lead to a rigged election

A

President Trump has reacted a lot to the mail-in ballots.

TRUMP'S G.S.

Yes.

A

More states are choosing to do universal mail-in voting. Mr. Trump has criticized that it is not good. Some are voicing that it will rig the election for the Democrats.

TRUMP'S G.S.

Sure. I am also considering a plan to make that void, just in case. If, in the slightest chance, they...

Where was it recently? In Belarus or somewhere, there was an election that was not free and fair. The winner got 80 percent of the votes, but the EU admitted that this was false. They rejected the election results.

A

Right.

TRUMP'S G.S.

Electoral fraud happens. It really does. It is because it takes more people to handle the ballots when they come in by mail.

I do not want to sound like I am saying there are illiterate people in the U.S., but with mail-in ballots, someone else could vote instead of you. Someone could fill out a bunch of ballots and send them in without anyone being able to verify their identity. That is why I am skeptical.

China's real vital point that Biden cannot resolve

A

Certainly, there will be these variables. I have a feeling you have something that you can do to bring the public opinion to your side, in a way that everyone can see.

TRUMP'S G.S.

Well... China is in a disastrous state right now. I will make this known to the world in some way. Also, there is a criminal act China is committing against the U.S. that I have not made public yet.

A

Is there?

TRUMP'S G.S.

When I reveal it, everyone will be shocked at how terrible a country China is, and it's something that Biden cannot resolve.

A

But you can?

TRUMP'S G.S.

Absolutely. I still have it in my hand. I have not played their real vital point yet. Biden cannot resolve it.

A

Do you know their vital point?

TRUMP'S G.S.

Right. Biden will not be able to resolve it.

A

Does it involve Biden?

TRUMP'S G.S.

Yes. Biden is already bribed, so he will not be able to do anything about it. He cannot. So, when I have to show that I am the only one that can do it, I can show it.

A

I see.

TRUMP'S G.S.

What else? Oh, they seem to want to label me a racist, etc. Out of desperation, they are calling me all kinds of things. China is giving out money to instigate the riots. I know that.

Ultimately, the fact that they infected nearly six million with the virus and caused the deaths of well over 100,000 Americans amounts to an act of war. Eventually, when I disclose what I know and when people see that I am acting as a wartime president in a time of national emergency, the tide will turn.

A
I see.

4

Expectations for Happy Science

Systems that uphold freedom, democracy, and faith should be kept mainstream in the world

A

We intend to translate this book into English to support President Trump. Is there another issue that we should cover and include?

TRUMP'S G.S.

Hmm. I have to be careful not to slip up. I'm being like Biden [*laughs*].

A

[*Laughs.*]

TRUMP'S G.S.

I am in a position where I cannot make a slip-up, so...

A

Yes, since the presidential race is a sensitive topic.

TRUMP'S G.S.

Hmm. Hey madam (Aide to Master & CEO Shio Okawa), help me out here. Tell me, is there anything I should say? You are always so thoughtful.

SHIO OKAWA

Hmm... Mr. C?

TRUMP'S G.S.

Ah, Mr. C.

A

What do you think, Mr. C?

TRUMP'S G.S.

Mr. C, how do I win? Advise me.

C

Ah... I would like to get your comment on one matter.

President Trump is, as Master Ryuho Okawa has found through his spiritual investigation, the reincarnation of George Washington[*], the hero who achieved the American

---

[*] See *The Trump Secret* on p.14.

Revolution. If the present day amounts to what the American Revolution was then, what more is to come, or what more will you make happen?

TRUMP'S G.S.

Well, Master Ryuho Okawa has spoken about that too. At the very least, we, meaning Master Okawa and myself, want to fulfill our responsibility of keeping systems that uphold freedom, democracy, and faith mainstream in the world, not just through the 21st century, but into the 22nd century as well.

I want to make such international systems, to get the world going in that direction, and to get countries that will be making progress from now on to be a part of that trend. In this respect, we must block China's way of thinking with a "Great Wall."

Faith is important too, you know. Japanese politicians do not talk about faith, but this is atrocious. They imitate our freedom and democracy, but they are missing the most important thing: faith in God. Without it, they have nothing to stop them from doing all kinds of bad things behind closed doors.

Pro-Chinese politicians in Japan and their corruption scandals

TRUMP'S G.S.

Japanese politicians wheel and deal under the table while, on the outside, they say the most meaningless things to keep the mass media off their backs and deceive their people, right?

I bet those Japanese prominent figures who are pro-China are receiving a lot of money from China. Biden is not the only one.

A

Like Mr. Nikai?

TRUMP'S G.S.

They are getting a lot of money and support. Many of them have been given women too. They have been taken in so tightly that there is no escaping. China has been planting traps for years, since the 1990s.

We actually have a hold of a lot of corruption scandals of these Japanese politicians. If I do not have to make use of them, I will not.

A

Please use them.

TRUMP'S G.S.

But if there is a need for them, there is a way to leak them to the Japanese media through different routes...

A

Please leak them from the U.S. side.

TRUMP'S G.S.

OK. We will reduce the number of pro-Chinese politicians. They are colluding with China and doing a lot of bad things.

A

They include Prime Minister Abe's aides.

TRUMP'S G.S.

Yes. At the source is another connection, the Japanese ruling party's coalition with the Komeito Party. That party, SGI (Soka Gakkai), and China are secretly connected. We know this. They are leading the pro-China movement on the grassroots level, spreading in Japan the idea that China's prosperity brings peace. Prime Minister Abe cannot act freely as though he is entangled in those vines.

A

You are right. Recently, those for a liberal system who escape China and come to this country are discovering that Japan is full of Chinese spies. They have to move on to other countries because it is dangerous here.

TRUMP'S G.S.

Exactly. Your Happiness Realization Party (HRP) is struggling because Japan is full of fake news media too. But I hope you will make a breakthrough.

Trump overcame obstacles with his never-give-up spirit and positive thinking

TRUMP'S G.S.

Japan needs fixing on a fundamental level. For democracy to work, you have to allow public disclosure of information and freedom of speech and expression.

It is tough for me too. It is not like I know what every police officer is doing. A white police officer suffocated an African American to death by kneeling on his neck... Maybe he broke his neck, I do not know. But the news was everywhere.

Under Xi Jinping, that news would never have been reported and everyone involved would have been gotten rid of. He surely would. Anyone who is involved or knows the truth would be gotten rid of. Anybody with the data would all disappear.

I want people to know that our system which refrains from doing that and allows information to be disclosed is a wonderful system.

A
Right.

TRUMP'S G.S.
A country that allows information to be disclosed even if it is unfavorable to its leader is a fair country, and a president who can still fight and win even when such unfavorable news is disclosed is a great president. I want people to know that.

I also experienced my real estate business going under when Japan's bubble economy burst and the financial crisis hit. I had to restructure my company after the Lehman Brothers collapsed.

Luckily, Dr. Norman Vincent Peale taught me when I was young, so I was able to build it up from scratch again with my never-give-up spirit. It is quite hard for Japanese people to believe, but I am now the American president with personal assets valuing in the billions. I did not make them through fraudulent means. I have made a comeback from the brink of bankruptcy and continue to overcome things with my positive thinking.

Dr. Peale talks about this. Mr. Ryuho Okawa and I are the same. We both had nothing to our name, but fought for and achieved great success. This is because we know the power of the mind. Especially, the kind of thought that is congratulated by God and is positive and constructive will always win in the end. I am building a wall between the U.S. and Mexico, but on the other hand, I will bring down the Great Wall of China.

The Chinese government only cares about the Han ethnic group. They are racist. Basically, they do not care if ethnicities other than the Hans are made slaves, right? I plan on crushing that idea.

"Master Ryuho Okawa and I are fellow heroes, we think alike"

TRUMP'S G.S.

Biden will only spin the media with his left-wing words. I, on the other hand, will fight by speaking my honest thoughts.

When there is a crisis, you have to stage a comeback. Look at Rocky. He always gets close to being knocked out, but he pushes on and finally wins in the final round. That is what makes him a hero. It is not always a good thing for the opponent to be knocked out with one punch. Sometimes you need to be cornered. You have to have a crisis.

A

You really are an American hero in your nature.

TRUMP'S G.S.

The American hero. I am an American hero too.

A

You are right.

TRUMP'S G.S.

Master Ryuho Okawa is the Japanese hero. He is a hero. As fellow heroes, we think alike.

I do not think I will lose, but in the slight chance that I might, I believe it is possible that heaven will send its help or there will be help from the universe.

The connection between God Shiva and President Trump

B

The other day, in "Spiritual Messages from God Shiva*," there was mention that you and God Shiva are spiritually connected...

TRUMP'S G.S.

Well, right now I am bringing India to our side. China foresees that once the U.S. falls, their next opponent will be India. We will not fall, but they see India as their potential enemy and are beginning their attack on them.

You have sounded the warning bell about this too, but they made Nepal create a communist regime. They have

---

* See the aforementioned *Shiva-Shin-no-Me-kara-Mita-Chikyuu-no-Mirai-Keikaku*.

encroached on Bhutan and occupied them. In Kashmir, on Indian territory, they are building sheds and sending their people to live there. It is an ugly strategy of taking territory like slicing a salami, piece by piece, as an established fact.

We need to involve India in this properly too, so I am keeping a good relationship with God Shiva.

B

Do you mean that Mr. Trump's soul is one part of God Shiva's soul or body of energy?

TRUMP'S G.S.

Now, now, now [*laughs*], that is... I am not sure if that will make me look good or look bad. Madam, what do you think? What should I say?

SHIO OKAWA

You are friends, I guess.

B

You are friends.

TRUMP'S G.S.

Ah, friends [*laughs*].

A

[*Laughs.*]

TRUMP'S G.S.

We are friends. I am not God Shiva himself.

A

I understand. We will keep that a taboo.

TRUMP'S G.S.

Friends.

"Write 'God chose Mr. Trump as the president of the U.S.' on the wraparound band"

A

We have to wrap up now. We are genuinely trying to do everything we can in the next three months to help President Trump be reelected. Can you tell us what you would like for Happy Science or the HRP to do?

TRUMP'S G.S.

Thanks to you, the anti-Trump groups in Japan have weakened considerably. Before, they used to simply translate the American newspapers and TV news coverage and say that Hillary would win in a landslide. Right? Scholars and media outlets were all saying that. But Happy Science pushed a lot for Trump and now the media has warmed up to him a bit. It has gotten a lot better.

Just write on the wraparound band of this book, "God chose Mr. Trump as the president of the U.S." That will be enough.

A

On the book? OK.

TRUMP'S G.S.

Yes. God chose.

A

Right. God chose.

TRUMP'S G.S.

Yes, yes. Right. "Mr. Trump can still do it."

In exchange, when I get reelected, just as Nishi-no-shima Island resurfaced, the effort to bring the HRP up...

A
Yes, we need to make the effort.

TRUMP'S G.S.
I will make the effort to make that happen.

A
Oh, you will?

TRUMP'S G.S.
Yes.

A
Thank you.

TRUMP'S G.S.
Do not underestimate American power. We, too, have the power to influence Japan.

The U.S. will take on the role of punishing everything that is putting you at a disadvantage or restricting you.

I know of your work. Not only are you trying to protect Taiwan, but Hong Kong too. We think the same.

Trump's G.S. believes he is God's right hand or left hand

TRUMP'S G.S.

If I am reelected, I am thinking of changing the presidential term limits to a life term. Amending the constitution to set the presidency to a life term is worth a shot. I mean, if the person has been chosen by God, then that's how it should be, I think.

A

I agree. The one who is receiving God's Will exactly as it is, is President Trump...

TRUMP'S G.S.

Yes, I receive it straightforwardly. Word for word, down to the tiniest detail.

A

This is a political system above democracy...

TRUMP'S G.S.

Right. I feel that the work of both the HRP and Happy Science is completely identical to what I am doing as if we are the same down to every single finger. I am practically acting as God's right hand or left hand. I really feel that way.

Maybe, by pushing for me, you will be able to break through the last wall as a religion.

A

You are right.

TRUMP'S G.S.

Yes, I believe so.

What a Japanese leader must be able to say

TRUMP'S G.S.

The Japanese media will continue to praise Biden probably until the day of the election. They like to make people think Trump is losing. They love doing that, but I have a lot of cards to play.

When I run out of cards, I am sure Master Ryuho Okawa will drag out the dragon and tear it apart. I hope he will act as the Godzilla of Japan.

Japanese people are so indecisive. They cannot even talk about God's justice. I said to keep the churches open even during the coronavirus pandemic, but there isn't anyone in Japan who can say something like that, is there?

Even regarding the economy, the only person who truly sees what should be done is Master Ryuho Okawa. All the politicians are useless. The people are hopeless too, thanks to all the mass media leaning to the left. China is no longer left-wing, but Adolf Hitler's Nazi Party.

A
Right.

TRUMP'S G.S.
Japan has to realize that. Japan is saying that they occupied their neighbors and did not do good things, so every year on August 15, the emperor and other figures are pledging they will never have another war again, but do not be stupid. If Japan is about to be occupied, you have to fight against that.

Do not yield to an evil power. The symbol of Japan should not be doing that.

"We should never be envoys of evil and wage war to invade others. But we will defend in order to stop evil, and push back evil, and protect world peace. To that end, we will resolutely defend our territories, waters, and airspace, as well as the lives, property, and rights of our people." If you cannot say this, you have no right to be Japan's leader.

In my eyes, neither the prime minister nor the emperor is Japan's leader. I hear Mr. Abe gave up going to his summer house and kept his mouth shut for 50 days. He does not know what to do. So, like Biden, he holed himself up. He knew that any unnecessary move he makes will cause the Japanese economy to collapse.

It will be the end of Japan if you make Tokyo Governor Koike the prime minister. The same thing will happen as when Biden becomes president. She will be all about dealing with the coronavirus. It will be as if the minister of health became prime minister.

If the media cannot distinguish someone who can see the whole picture from someone who cannot, it'll be better without them. The level of the Japanese media is so low. The good, sensible opinions of Happy Science should be spread more and more.

I will pay you back double. Yes, I will pay you back double. So, for the next three months, I am counting on you.

A
Yes. I understand. Thank you very much for today.

TRUMP'S G.S.
OK.

5

The Words of God: "The Current Chinese Regime Will Fall"

RYUHO OKAWA

[*Claps three times*]. So, we heard them. We conducted this in Japanese, so that our members and believers as well as our Japanese members overseas can read and watch it. I would also like to see subtitles quickly made, so that the opinions of their guardian spirits can reach more people.

I have no intention of simply abandoning the people of Hong Kong. I will never forsake the people of Taiwan, either. As I promised in Canada*, I intend to liberate the

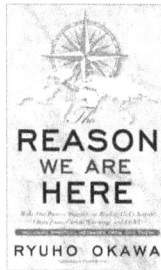

---

* The author held a lecture and Q&A session titled, "The Reason We Are Here" on October 6, 2019 in Toronto, Canada. See Ryuho Okawa, *The Reason We Are Here* (Tokyo: HS Press, 2020).

people of Uyghur, Southern Mongolia, and Tibet. I fully intend to liberate them and to bring the current Chinese regime down. These are the words of God, so that is how it will be.

Japan is resorting to cheap tricks like not letting the HRP be an official political party or refusing the approval of the Happy Science University under the pretext that spiritual messages are not academic. But I think an ogre's iron bat will strike their heads from a higher perspective.

I would very much like for Mr. Trump to be reelected and for him to step foot on Japanese soil again. That is all.

A

Thank you very much.

Afterword

To be honest, after comparing the opinions of the guardian spirits, maybe the world and Japan should have Trump be reelected.

Regarding the "China Virus," the left-wing media outlets and pro-Chinese activists around the world are working behind the scenes to make the idea of natural occurrence or the idea of simultaneous and worldwide outbreaks, the majority thinking. However, we cannot acknowledge opinions given by current China, considering they do not disclose information and do not allow freedom of speech. It is hard to believe that the virology laboratory in Wuhan was not involved with the spreading of the bat-borne coronavirus, which they had been researching for about 15 years. We cannot exclude the possibility that it was used as a weapon.

If Biden is elected president, China could become the next hegemonic power. We pray that the American citizens tell apart a creative statesman from a dictator and make the right choice.

Ryuho Okawa
Master & CEO of Happy Science Group
August 19, 2020

ABOUT THE AUTHOR

RYUHO OKAWA was born on July 7th 1956, in Tokushima, Japan. After graduating from the University of Tokyo with a law degree, he joined a Tokyo-based trading house. While working at its New York headquarters, he studied international finance at the Graduate Center of the City University of New York. In 1981, he attained Great Enlightenment and became aware that he is El Cantare with a mission to bring salvation to all of humankind. In 1986, he established Happy Science. It now has members in over 110 countries across the world, with more than 700 local branches and temples as well as 10,000 missionary houses around the world. The total number of lectures has exceeded 3,150 (of which more than 150 are in English) and over 2,700 books (of which more than 550 are Spiritual Interview Series) have been published, many of which are translated into 31 languages. Many of the books, including *The Laws of the Sun* have become best sellers or million sellers. To date, Happy Science has produced 20 movies. The original story and original concept were given by the Executive Producer Ryuho Okawa. Recent movie titles are *The Real Exorcist* (live-action, May 2020), *Living in the Age of Miracles* (documentary, Aug. 2020), and *Twiceborn* (live-action, scheduled to be released in Oct. 2020). He has also composed the lyrics and music of over 150 songs, such as theme songs and featured songs of movies. Moreover, he is the Founder of Happy Science University and Happy Science Academy (Junior and Senior High School), Founder and President of the Happiness Realization Party, Founder and Honorary Headmaster of Happy Science Institute of Government and Management, Founder of IRH Press Co., Ltd., and the Chairperson of New Star Production Co., Ltd. and ARI Production Co., Ltd.

WHAT IS EL CANTARE?

El Cantare means "the Light of the Earth," and is the Supreme God of the Earth who has been guiding humankind since the beginning of Genesis. He is whom Jesus called Father and Muhammad called Allah. Different parts of El Cantare's core consciousness have descended to Earth in the past, once as Alpha and another as Elohim. His branch spirits, such as Shakyamuni Buddha and Hermes, have descended to Earth many times and helped to flourish many civilizations. To unite various religions and to integrate various fields of study in order to build a new civilization on Earth, a part of the core consciousness has descended to Earth as Master Ryuho Okawa.

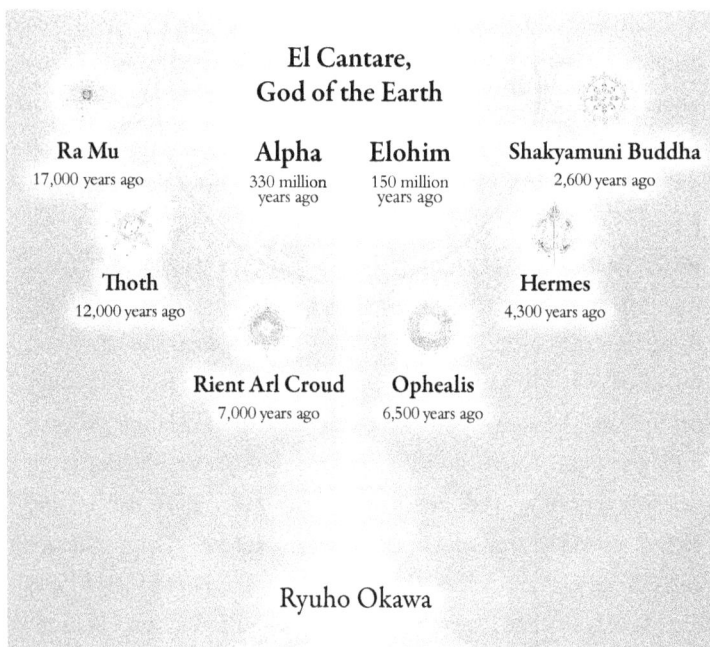

El Cantare,
God of the Earth

Ra Mu
17,000 years ago

Alpha
330 million
years ago

Elohim
150 million
years ago

Shakyamuni Buddha
2,600 years ago

Thoth
12,000 years ago

Hermes
4,300 years ago

Rient Arl Croud
7,000 years ago

Ophealis
6,500 years ago

Ryuho Okawa

Alpha is a part of the core consciousness of El Cantare who descended to Earth around 330 million years ago. Alpha preached Earth's Truths to harmonize and unify Earth-born humans and space people who came from other planets.

Elohim is a part of El Cantare's core consciousness who descended to Earth around 150 million years ago. He gave wisdom, mainly on the differences of light and darkness, good and evil.

Shakyamuni Buddha was born as a prince into the Shakya Clan in India around 2,600 years ago. When he was 29 years old, he renounced the world and sought enlightenment. He later attained Great Enlightenment and founded Buddhism.

Hermes is one of the 12 Olympian gods in Greek mythology, but the spiritual Truth is that he taught the teachings of love and progress around 4,300 years ago that became the origin of the current Western civilization. He is a hero that truly existed.

Ophealis was born in Greece around 6,500 years ago and was the leader who took an expedition to as far as Egypt. He is the God of miracles, prosperity, and arts, and is known as Osiris in the Egyptian mythology.

Rient Arl Croud was born as a king of the ancient Incan Empire around 7,000 years ago and taught about the mysteries of the mind. In the heavenly world, he is responsible for the interactions that take place between various planets.

Thoth was an almighty leader who built the golden age of the Atlantic civilization around 12,000 years ago. In the Egyptian mythology, he is known as god Thoth.

Ra Mu was a leader who built the golden age of the civilization of Mu around 17,000 years ago. As a religious leader and a politician, he ruled by uniting religion and politics.

WHAT IS A SPIRITUAL MESSAGE?

We are all spiritual beings living on this earth. The following is the mechanism behind Master Ryuho Okawa's spiritual messages.

1 You are a spirit

People are born into this world to gain wisdom through various experiences and return to the other world when their lives end. We are all spirits and repeat this cycle in order to refine our souls.

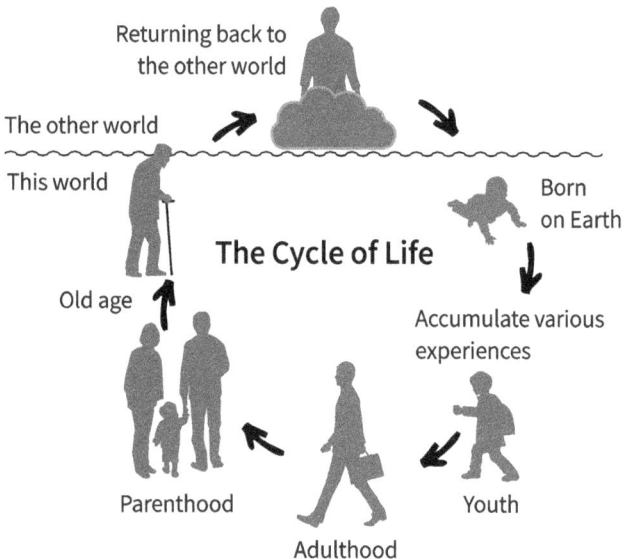

Returning back to
the other world

The other world

This world

Born
on Earth

The Cycle of Life

Old age

Accumulate various
experiences

Parenthood

Youth

Adulthood

2 You have a guardian spirit

Guardian spirits are those who protect the people who are living on this earth. Each of us has a guardian spirit that watches over us and guides us from the other world. They were us in our past life, and are identical in how we think.

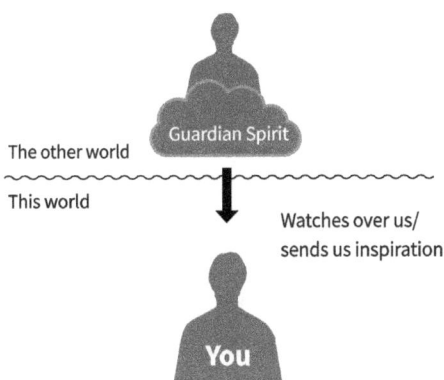

The other world

This world

Guardian Spirit

Watches over us/
sends us inspiration

You

3 How spiritual messages work

Master Ryuho Okawa, through his enlightenment, is capable of summoning any spirit from anywhere in the world, including the spirit world.

Master Okawa's way of receiving spiritual messages is fundamentally different from that of other psychic mediums who undergo trances and are thereby completely taken over by the spirits they are channeling.

Master Okawa's attainment of a high level of enlightenment enables him to retain full control of his consciousness and body throughout the duration of the spiritual message. To allow the spirits to express their own thoughts and personalities freely, however, Master Okawa usually softens the dominancy of his consciousness. This way, he is able to keep his own philosophies out of the way and ensure that the spiritual messages are pure expressions of the spirits he is channeling.

Since guardian spirits think at the same subconscious level as the person living on earth, Master Okawa can summon the spirit and find out what the person on earth is actually thinking. If the person has already returned to the other world, the spirit can give messages to the people living on earth through Master Okawa.

Since 2009, more than 1,100 sessions of spiritual messages have been openly recorded by Master Okawa, and the majority of these have been published. Spiritual messages from the guardian spirits of people living today such as Donald Trump, Japanese Prime Minister Shinzo Abe and Chinese President Xi Jinping, as well as spiritual messages sent from the spirit world by Jesus Christ, Muhammad, Thomas Edison, Mother Teresa, Steve Jobs and Nelson Mandela are just a tiny pack of spiritual messages that were published so far.

Domestically, in Japan, these spiritual messages are being read by a wide range of politicians and mass media, and the high-level contents of these books are delivering an impact even more on politics, news and public opinion. In recent years, there have been spiritual messages recorded in English, and English translations are being done on the spiritual messages given in Japanese. These have been published overseas, one after another, and have started to shake the world.

1 The guardian spirit / spirit in the other world...

2 Goes inside Master Okawa in this world

3 Master Okawa speaks the words of the guardian spirit / spirit

For more about spiritual messages and a complete list of books in the Spiritual Interview Series, visit __okawabooks.com__

ABOUT HAPPY SCIENCE

Happy Science is a global movement that empowers individuals to find purpose and spiritual happiness and to share that happiness with their families, societies, and the world. With more than 12 million members around the world, Happy Science aims to increase awareness of spiritual truths and expand our capacity for love, compassion, and joy so that together we can create the kind of world we all wish to live in.

Activities at Happy Science are based on the Principles of Happiness (Love, Wisdom, Self-Reflection, and Progress). These principles embrace worldwide philosophies and beliefs, transcending boundaries of culture and religions.

Love teaches us to give ourselves freely without expecting anything in return; it encompasses giving, nurturing, and forgiving.

Wisdom leads us to the insights of spiritual truths, and opens us to the true meaning of life and the will of God (the universe, the highest power, Buddha).

Self-Reflection brings a mindful, nonjudgmental lens to our thoughts and actions to help us find our truest selves—the essence of our souls—and deepen our connection to the highest power. It helps us attain a clean and peaceful mind and leads us to the right life path.

Progress emphasizes the positive, dynamic aspects of our spiritual growth—actions we can take to manifest and spread happiness around the world. It's a path that not only expands our soul growth, but also furthers the collective potential of the world we live in.

PROGRAMS AND EVENTS

The doors of Happy Science are open to all. We offer a variety of programs and events, including self-exploration and self-growth programs, spiritual seminars, meditation and contemplation sessions, study groups, and book events.

Our programs are designed to:
* Deepen your understanding of your purpose and meaning in life
* Improve your relationships and increase your capacity to love unconditionally
* Attain peace of mind, decrease anxiety and stress, and feel positive
* Gain deeper insights and a broader perspective on the world
* Learn how to overcome life's challenges
  ... and much more.

*For more information, visit **happy-science.org**.*

OUR ACTIVITIES

Happy Science does other various activities to provide support for those in need.

◆ **You Are An Angel! General Incorporated Association**

Happy Science has a volunteer network in Japan that encourages and supports children with disabilities as well as their parents and guardians.

◆ **Never Mind School for Truancy**

At 'Never Mind,' we support students who find it very challenging to attend schools in Japan. We also nurture their self-help spirit and power to rebound against obstacles in life based on Master Okawa's teachings and faith.

◆ **"Prevention Against Suicide" Campaign since 2003**

A nationwide campaign to reduce suicides; over 20,000 people commit suicide every year in Japan. "The Suicide Prevention Website-Words of Truth for You-" presents spiritual prescriptions for worries such as depression, lost love, extramarital affairs, bullying and work-related problems, thereby saving many lives.

◆ **Support for Anti-bullying Campaigns**

Happy Science provides support for a group of parents and guardians, Network to Protect Children from Bullying, a general incorporated foundation launched in Japan to end bullying, including those that can even be called a criminal offense. So far, the network received more than 5,000 cases and resolved 90% of them.

◆ The Golden Age Scholarship

This scholarship is granted to students who can contribute greatly and bring a hopeful future to the world.

◆ Success No.1
Buddha's Truth Afterschool Academy

Happy Science has over 180 classrooms throughout Japan and in several cities around the world that focus on afterschool education for children. The education focuses on faith and morals in addition to supporting children's school studies.

◆ Angel Plan V

For children under the age of kindergarten, Happy Science holds classes for nurturing healthy, positive, and creative boys and girls.

◆ Future Stars Training Department

The Future Stars Training Department was founded within the Happy Science Media Division with the goal of nurturing talented individuals to become successful in the performing arts and entertainment industry.

◆ New Star Production Co., Ltd.
ARI Production Co., Ltd.

We have companies to nurture actors and actresses, artists, and vocalists. They are also involved in film production.

DOCUMENTARY MOVIE
HEART TO HEART

In this documentary movie, Happy Science University students visit these NPO activities to discover what salvation truly is, and on the meaning of life, through heart-to-heart interviews.

TWICEBORN

Coming to Theaters Fall 2020

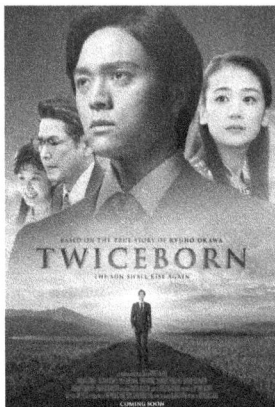

STORY In July 1991, Satoru Ichijo is about to give a lecture in Tokyo Dome. The media pays attention to him as a "Great Charisma." Time goes back to a spring day right before the college graduation, Satoru receives a message from the spiritual world and realizes he has a mission to lead humankind to happiness. While he has constant contact with the spiritual world, Satoru becomes a successful businessman. One day, spirits tell him an overwhelming mission. "Your mission as the Buddha reborn, is to save all people by spreading the Truth." Satoru tries to rise up to fulfill his mission, but his decision is shaken by the devil's temptation. In solitude, Satoru chooses to live his mission as "Savior", leaves everything behind including his loved one, and steps out onto the stage of Tokyo dome...

LIVING IN THE AGE OF MIRACLES

A documentary film to be released in Aug. 2020

An inspirational documentary about two Japanese actors meeting people who experienced miracles in their lives. Through their quest, they find the key to working miracles and learn what "living in the age of miracles" truly means.

6 Awards from USA!

WINNER
AWARD OF MERIT
SPECIAL MENTION
IMPACT DOCS AWARDS

GOLD AWARD
Documentary Feature
International
Independent Film Awards
Spring 2020

GOLD AWARD
Concept
International
Independent Film Awards
Spring 2020

...and more!

IMMORTAL HERO   On VOD NOW

Based on the true story of a man whose near death experience inspires him
to choose life... and change the lives of millions.

40 Awards from 9 Countries!

SPAIN
BARCELONA INTERNATIONAL
FILM FESTIVAL 2019
[THE CASTELL AWARDS]

SPAIN
MADRID INTERNATIONAL
FILM FESTIVAL 2019
[BEST DIRECTOR OF A FOREIGN
LANGUAGE FEATURE FILM]

ITALY
FLORENCE FILM AWARDS JUL 2019
[HONORABLE MENTION:
FEATURE FILM]

USA
INDIE VISIONS FILM FESTIVAL
JUL 2019 [WINNER (NARRATIVE
FEATURE FILM)]

ITALY
FLORENCE FILM AWARDS JUL 2019
[BEST ORIGINAL SCREENPLAY]

ITALY
DIAMOND FILM AWARDS JUL 2019
[WINNER (NARRATIVE
FEATURE FILM)]

...and more!

For more information, visit **www.immortal-hero.com**

THE REAL EXORCIST

55 Awards from 8 Countries!

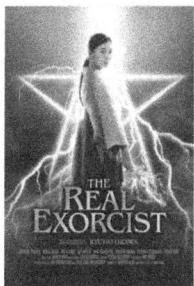

STORY Tokyo —the most mystical city in the world where
you find spiritual spots in the most unexpected places. Sayuri
works as a part time waitress at a small coffee shop "Extra"
where regular customers enjoy the authentic coffee that the
owner brews. Meanwhile, Sayuri uses her supernatural powers
to help those who are troubled by spiritual phenomena one
after another. Through her special consultations, she touches
the hearts of the people and helps them by showing the truths
of the invisible world.

USA
GOLD REMI AWARD
53rd WorldFest Houston
International Film Festival 2020

MONACO
BEST FEATURE FILM
17th Angel Film Awards
2020
Monaco International Film Festival

BEST FEMALE ACTOR
17th Angel Film Awards
2020
Monaco International Film Festival

NIGERIA
BEST FEATURE FILM
EKO International Film Festival
2020

BEST FEMALE SUPPORTING ACTOR
17th Angel Film Awards
2020
Monaco International Film Festival

BEST SUPPORTING ACTRESS
EKO International Film Festival
2020

BEST VISUAL EFFECTS
17th Angel Film Awards
2020
Monaco International Film Festival

...and more!

For more information, visit **www.realexorcistmovie.com**

CONTACT INFORMATION

Happy Science is a worldwide organization with faith centers around the globe. For a comprehensive list of centers, visit the worldwide directory at *happy-science.org*. The following are some of the many Happy Science locations:

UNITED STATES AND CANADA

New York
79 Franklin St., New York, NY 10013
Phone: 212-343-7972
Fax: 212-343-7973
Email: ny@happy-science.org
Website: happyscience-na.org

Los Angeles
1590 E. Del Mar Blvd., Pasadena, CA 91106
Phone: 626-395-7775
Fax: 626-395-7776
Email: la@happy-science.org
Website: happyscience-na.org

New Jersey
725 River Rd, #102B, Edgewater, NJ 07020
Phone: 201-313-0127
Fax: 201-313-0120
Email: nj@happy-science.org
Website: happyscience-na.org

Orange County
10231 Slater Ave., #204
Fountain Valley, CA 92708
Phone: 714-745-1140
Email: oc@happy-science.org
Website: happyscience-na.org

Florida
5208 8th St., St. Zephyrhills, FL 33542
Phone: 813-715-0000
Fax: 813-715-0010
Email: florida@happy-science.org
Website: happyscience-na.org

San Diego
7841 Balboa Ave., Suite #202
San Diego, CA 92111
Phone: 619-381-7615
Fax: 626-395-7776
E-mail: sandiego@happy-science.org
Website: happyscience-na.org

Atlanta
1874 Piedmont Ave., NE Suite 360-C
Atlanta, GA 30324
Phone: 404-892-7770
Email: atlanta@happy-science.org
Website: happyscience-na.org

Hawaii
Phone: 808-591-9772
Fax: 808-591-9776
Email: hi@happy-science.org
Website: happyscience-na.org

San Francisco
525 Clinton St.
Redwood City, CA 94062
Phone & Fax: 650-363-2777
Email: sf@happy-science.org
Website: happyscience-na.org

Kauai
3343 Kanakolu Street, Suite 5
Lihue, HI 96766, U.S.A.
Phone: 808-822-7007
Fax: 808-822-6007
Email: kauai-hi@happy-science.org
Website: kauai.happyscience-na.org

Toronto
845 The Queensway
Etobicoke ON M8Z 1N6 Canada
Phone: 1-416-901-3747
Email: toronto@happy-science.org
Website: happy-science.ca

Vancouver
#201-2607 East 49th Avenue
Vancouver, BC, V5S 1J9, Canada
Phone: 1-604-437-7735
Fax: 1-604-437-7764
Email: vancouver@happy-science.org
Website: happy-science.ca

INTERNATIONAL

Tokyo
1-6-7 Togoshi, Shinagawa
Tokyo, 142-0041 Japan
Phone: 81-3-6384-5770
Fax: 81-3-6384-5776
Email: tokyo@happy-science.org
Website: happy-science.org

Seoul
74, Sadang-ro 27-gil,
Dongjak-gu, Seoul, Korea
Phone: 82-2-3478-8777
Fax: 82-2-3478-9777
Email: korea@happy-science.org
Website: happyscience-korea.org

London
3 Margaret St.
London,W1W 8RE United Kingdom
Phone: 44-20-7323-9255
Fax: 44-20-7323-9344
Email: eu@happy-science.org
Website: happyscience-uk.org

Taipei
No. 89, Lane 155, Dunhua N. Road
Songshan District, Taipei City 105, Taiwan
Phone: 886-2-2719-9377
Fax: 886-2-2719-5570
Email: taiwan@happy-science.org
Website: happyscience-tw.org

Sydney
516 Pacific Hwy, Lane Cove North,
NSW 2066, Australia
Phone: 61-2-9411-2877
Fax: 61-2-9411-2822
Email: sydney@happy-science.org

Malaysia
No 22A, Block 2, Jalil Link Jalan Jalil Jaya 2,
Bukit Jalil 57000, Kuala Lumpur, Malaysia
Phone: 60-3-8998-7877
Fax: 60-3-8998-7977
Email: malaysia@happy-science.org
Website: happyscience.org.my

Brazil Headquarters
Rua. Domingos de Morais 1154,
Vila Mariana, Sao Paulo SP
CEP 04009-002, Brazil
Phone: 55-11-5088-3800
Fax: 55-11-5088-3806
Email: sp@happy-science.org
Website: happyscience.com.br

Nepal
Kathmandu Metropolitan City Ward
No. 15,
Ring Road, Kimdol,
Sitapaila Kathmandu, Nepal
Phone: 97-714-272931
Email: nepal@happy-science.org

Jundiai
Rua Congo, 447, Jd. Bonfiglioli
Jundiai-CEP, 13207-340
Phone: 55-11-4587-5952
Email: jundiai@happy-science.org

Uganda
Plot 877 Rubaga Road, Kampala
P.O. Box 34130, Kampala, Uganda
Phone: 256-79-4682-121
Email: uganda@happy-science.org
Website: happyscience-uganda.org

ABOUT HAPPINESS REALIZATION PARTY

The Happiness Realization Party (HRP) was founded in May 2009 by Master Ryuho Okawa as part of the Happy Science Group to offer concrete and proactive solutions to the current issues such as military threats from North Korea and China and the long-term economic recession. HRP aims to implement drastic reforms of the Japanese government, thereby bringing peace and prosperity to Japan. To accomplish this, HRP proposes two key policies:

1) Strengthening the national security and the Japan-U.S. alliance, which plays a vital role in the stability of Asia.

2) Improving the Japanese economy by implementing drastic tax cuts, taking monetary easing measures and creating new major industries.

HRP advocates that Japan should offer a model of a religious nation that allows diverse values and beliefs to coexist, and that contributes to global peace.

*For more information, visit **en.hr-party.jp***

ABOUT IRH PRESS

IRH Press Co., Ltd., based in Tokyo, was founded in 1987 as a publishing division of Happy Science. IRH Press publishes religious and spiritual books, journals, magazines and also operates broadcast and film production enterprises. For more information, visit *okawabooks.com*.

Follow us on:

Facebook: Okawa Books   **Twitter**: Okawa Books
Goodreads: Ryuho Okawa   **Instagram**: OkawaBooks
Pinterest: Okawa Books

RYUHO OKAWA'S LAWS SERIES

The Laws Series is an annual volume of books that are mainly comprised of Ryuho Okawa's lectures on various topics that highlight principles and guidelines for the activities of Happy Science every year. *The Laws of the Sun*, the first publication of the Laws Series, ranked in the annual best-selling list in Japan. Since then, all of the Laws Series' titles have ranked in the annual best-selling list for more than two decades, setting sociocultural trends in Japan and around the world.

THE TRILOGY

The first three volumes of the Laws Series, *The Laws of the Sun*, *The Golden Laws*, and *The Nine Dimensions* make a trilogy that completes the basic framework of the teachings of God's Truths. *The Laws of the Sun* discusses the structure of God's Laws, *The Golden Laws* expounds on the doctrine of time, and *The Nine Dimensions* reveals the nature of space.

BOOKS BY RYUHO OKAWA

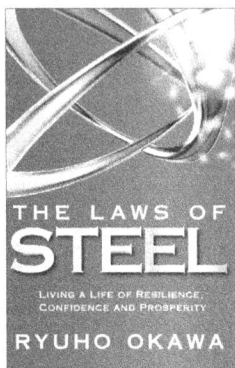

THE LAWS OF STEEL
LIVING A LIFE OF RESILIENCE, CONFIDENCE AND PROSPERITY

Paperback • 256 pages • $16.95
ISBN: 978-1-942125-65-5

This book is a compilation of six lectures that Ryuho Okawa gave in 2018 and 2019, each containing passionate messages for us to open a brighter future. This powerful and inspiring book will not only show us the ways to achieve true happiness and prosperity, but also the ways to solve many global issues we now face. It presents us with wisdom that is based on a spiritual perspective, and a new design for our future society. Through this book, we can overcome different values and create a peaceful world, thereby ushering in a Golden Age.

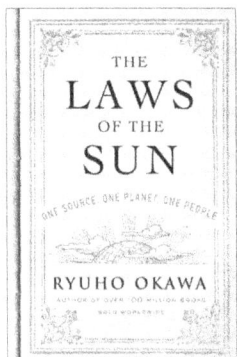

THE LAWS OF THE SUN
ONE SOURCE, ONE PLANET, ONE PEOPLE

Paperback • 288 pages • $15.95
ISBN: 978-1-942125-43-3

Imagine if you could ask God why he created this world and what spiritual laws he used to shape us—and everything around us. In *The Laws of the Sun*, Ryuho Okawa outlines these laws of the universe and provides a road map for living one's life with greater purpose and meaning. This powerful book shows the way to realize true happiness—a happiness that continues from this world through the other.

*For a complete list of books, visit **okawabooks.com***

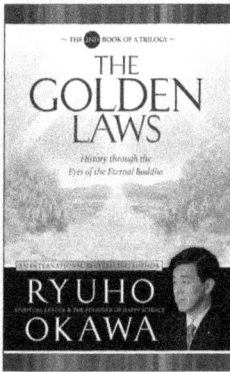

The Golden Laws
History through the Eyes of the Eternal Buddha

Paperback • 201 pages • $14.95
ISBN: 978-1-941779-81-1

Throughout history, Great Guiding Spirits of Light have been present on Earth in both the East and the West at crucial points in human history to further our spiritual development. *The Golden Laws* reveals how Divine Plan has been unfolding on Earth, and outlines 5,000 years of the secret history of humankind. Once we understand the true course of history, through past, present and into the future, we cannot help but become aware of the significance of our spiritual mission in the present age.

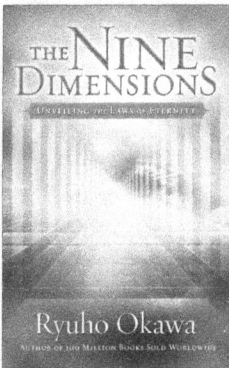

The Nine Dimensions
Unveiling the Laws of Eternity

Paperback • 168 pages • $15.95
ISBN: 978-0-982698-56-3

This book is a window into the mind of our loving God, who designed this world and the vast, wondrous world of our afterlife as a school with many levels through which our souls learn and grow. When the religions and cultures of the world discover the truth of their common spiritual origin, they will be inspired to accept their differences, come together under faith in God, and build an era of harmony and peaceful progress on Earth.

*For a complete list of books, visit **okawabooks.com***

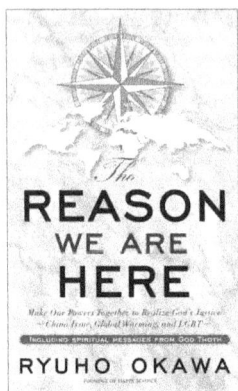

THE REASON WE ARE HERE

MAKE OUR POWERS TOGETHER TO REALIZE GOD'S JUSTICE -CHINA ISSUE, GLOBAL WARMING, AND LGBT-

Paperback • 215 pages • $14.95
ISBN: 978-1-943869-62-6

The Reason We Are Here is a book of thought that is unlike any other: its global perspective, timely opinion on current issues, and spiritual class are unmatched. The main content is the lecture in Toronto, Canada given in October 2019 by Ryuho Okawa, a Japanese spiritual leader and the national teacher of Japan. Also included are his answers to the questions—specifically, on the Hong Kong and Uyghur problems—from renowned activists who attended his lecture.

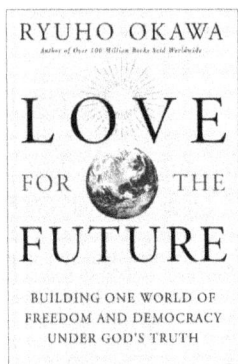

LOVE FOR THE FUTURE

BUILDING ONE WORLD OF FREEDOM AND DEMOCRACY UNDER GOD'S TRUTH

Paperback • 312 pages • $15.95
ISBN: 978-1-942125-60-0

This is a compilation of select international lectures given by Ryuho Okawa during his (ongoing) global missionary tours. While conflicting values of justice exists, this book espouses that freedom and democracy are vital principles for global unification that will resolutely foster peace and shared prosperity, if adopted universally.

For a complete list of books, visit ***okawabooks.com***

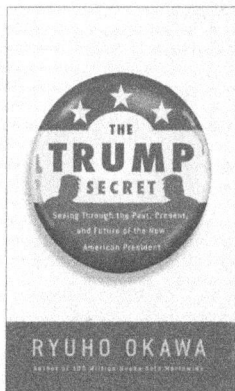

THE TRUMP SECRET
SEEING THROUGH THE PAST, PRESENT, AND FUTURE OF THE NEW AMERICAN PRESIDENT

Paperback • 208 pages • $14.95
ISBN: 978-1-942125-22-8

This book contains a series of lectures and interviews that unveil the secrets to Trump's victory and makes predictions of what will happen under his presidency. This book predicts the coming of a new America that will go through a great transformation from the "red and blue states" to the United States.

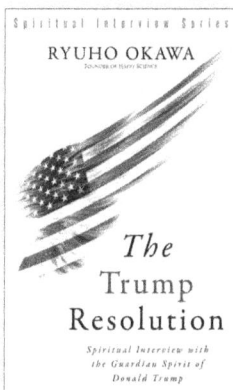

THE TRUMP RESOLUTION
SPIRITUAL INTERVIEW WITH THE GUARDIAN SPIRIT OF DONALD TRUMP

Paperback • 104 pages • $9.95
ISBN: 978-1-943869-38-1

This is a spiritual interview with the guardian spirit of President Donald Trump, conducted through the spiritual power of Master Okawa of Happy Science on April 28, 2018, the day after the historic meeting between the North and South Korean leaders. What did President Trump want to achieve in the U.S.-North Korea summit on June 12, 2018? This is the one and only exclusive spiritual interview where you can find out his true thoughts.

*For a complete list of books, visit **okawabooks.com***

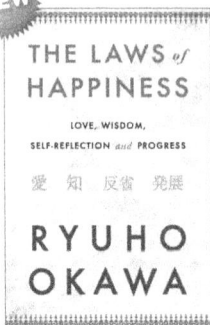

THE LAWS OF HAPPINESS

LOVE, WISDOM, SELF-REFLECTION AND
PROGRESS

Paperback • 264 pages • $16.95
ISBN: 978-1-942125-70-9

What is happiness? In this book, Ryuho Okawa explains
that happiness is not found outside us; it's found within
us, in how we think, how we look at our lives in this
world, what we believe in, and how we devote our hearts
to the work we do. Even as we go through suffering
and unfavorable circumstances, we can always shift
our mindset and become happier by simply *giving love*
instead of *taking love.*

THE REAL EXORCIST

ATTAIN WISDOM TO CONQUER EVIL

Paperback • 208 pages • $16.95
ISBN:978-1-942125-67-9

This is a profound spiritual text backed by the author's
nearly 40 years of real-life experience with spiritual
phenomena. In it, Okawa teaches how we may discern
and overcome our negative tendencies, by acquiring
the right knowledge, mindset and lifestyle.

THE LAWS OF JUSTICE

HOW WE CAN SOLVE WORLD CONFLICTS &
BRING PEACE

Paperback • 208 pages • $15.95
ISBN: 978-1-942125-05-1

This book shows what global justice is from a
comprehensive perspective of the Supreme God.
Becoming aware of this view will let us embrace
differences in beliefs, recognize other people's divine
nature, and love and forgive one another. It will also
become the key to solving religious, political, societal,
economic, or academic issues in order to build a better
and safer world for all of us.

---

*For a complete list of books, visit **okawabooks.com***

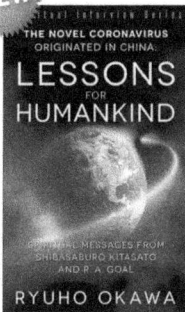

THE NOVEL CORONAVIRUS ORIGINATED IN CHINA: LESSONS FOR HUMANKIND

SPIRITUAL MESSAGES FROM SHIBASABURO KITASATO AND R. A. GOAL

Paperback • 228 pages • $13.95
ISBN: 978-1-943869-88-6

This book records spiritual messages from a bacteriologist and a space being. They disclose many truths about the novel coronavirus pandemic, such as China's hidden secrets, what the future holds, and hopeful messages for humanity. Only when humanity learns what we are to learn from this pandemic, can we escape this worldwide crisis and create a new age.

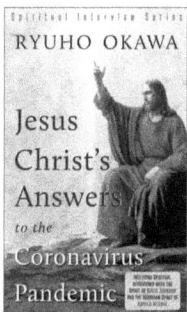

JESUS CHRIST'S ANSWERS TO THE CORONAVIRUS PANDEMIC

Paperback • 204 pages • $11.95
ISBN: 978-1-943869-81-7

In this book, the spirit of Jesus answers the causes, prospects, and coping strategies for the novel coronavirus pandemic. Instead of hoping for the development of an effective vaccine to come soon, we should use our spiritual power to defeat the evil thoughts that spiritually possess this virus. It's a book for all who believe in Jesus.

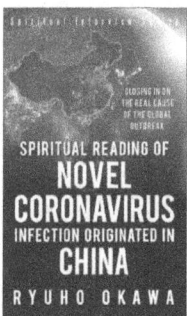

SPIRITUAL READING OF NOVEL CORONAVIRUS INFECTION ORIGINATED IN CHINA

CLOSING IN ON THE REAL CAUSE OF THE GLOBAL OUTBREAK

Paperback • 278 pages • $13.95
ISBN: 978-1-943869-77-0

This worldwide pandemic is not a mere act of nature nor a coincidence, but rather, heaven's warning to humanity, especially China. Through this book, you can find out "the immunity" against the novel coronavirus, among other shocking truths.

---

*For a complete list of books, visit **okawabooks.com***

SPIRITUAL INTERVIEW WITH THE GUARDIAN SPIRIT OF POPE FRANCIS
The Vatican Agonizes over the Coronavirus Pandemic

WHAT WILL BECOME OF CORONAVIRUS PANDEMIC?
Readings by Edgar Cayce

THE NEW RESURRECTION
My Miraculous Story of Overcoming Illness and Death

THE ROYAL ROAD OF LIFE
Beginning Your Path of Inner Peace, Virtue, and a Life of Purpose

THE LAWS OF GREAT ENLIGHTENMENT
Always Walk with Buddha

I CAN
Discover Your Power Within

THE STARTING POINT OF HAPPINESS
An Inspiring Guide to Positive Living with Faith, Love, and Courage

HEALING FROM WITHIN
Life-Changing Keys to Calm, Spiritual, and Healthy Living

SPIRITUAL WORLD 101
A Guide to a Spiritually Happy Life

*For a complete list of books, visit **okawabooks.com***